An Annotated Guide to
Basic Reference Books on the
Black American Experience

TO MY FAMILY

An Annotated Guide to Basic Reference Books on the Black American Experience

GUY T. WESTMORELAND, JR.

SR *Scholarly Resources Inc.*
Wilmington, Delaware • London

Published in 1974 by
SCHOLARLY RESOURCES, INC.
1508 Pennsylvania Avenue
Wilmington, Delaware 19806

Library of Congress Catalog Card Number: 74-79558
International Standard Book Number: 0-8420-1738-0

Printed and bound in the United States of America.

CONTENTS

Preface vii

PART ONE: GENERAL REFERENCE SOURCES 1

Bibliographic Guides and Catalogs of
Special Library Collections. 1

Biographical Sources 6

Dictionaries, Encyclopedias, Handbooks,
and Yearbooks. 11

Indexes to Periodical Literature 19

Multi-Subject Bibliographies 21

PART TWO: SUBJECT AREA REFERENCE SOURCES 33

Civil Rights and Black America 33

Drama, Fine Arts, Music and Sports 36

Economic Life and Business Affairs 40

Education. 41

History. 47

Literature and Folklore 53

Media (Press, Radio and Television). 60

Race Relations 63

Slavery. 65

Society and Culture. 66

ADDENDUM   74

AUTHOR INDEX   75

TITLE INDEX   82

SUBJECT INDEX   92

PREFACE

The title phrase, <u>Black American Experience</u>, is used
here to refer to the overall historical and contemporary
experiences (artistic, economic, political, social, etc.)
of Afro-Americans primarily in the United States, but also
in Canada, the West Indies, and Latin America. The primary
purpose of this guide is to organize and describe reference
books which deal primarily with this black American
experience although some of the titles included deal also
with the black experience in Africa and other parts of the
world. Furthermore, this is a selective guide to basic
reference sources, as described above, which have been
selected by this compiler.

While there are many reference books which serve as
useful aids in the study of the Afro-American experience,
this guide concentrates on those which deal primarily or
completely with that experience. The need for this kind
of guide has been generated by the emergence of Black
Studies as a separate discipline and the overall increased
desire to study the historical and contemporary impact of
blacks on American society.

The annotations of the material cited in this guide
attempt to bring out special features of each title. In

some cases this proved to be rather difficult to achieve because of the general nature of some of the titles, particularly some of the multi-subject bibliographies. In other cases, when the title was quite descriptive, the length of the annotation was limited. Heretofore, I have been unable to identify a similarly extensive annotated guide to reference books on Afro-Americans. It is hoped that this guide will aid students and scholars as well as librarians, bibliographers, and others working in African-American Studies and related disciplines.

The guide is divided into two major parts with Part One citing general reference sources and Part Two citing subject area reference sources. Part One is subdivided into categories which cite general reference works such as catalogs of special library collections, biographical sources, and multi-subject bibliographies. Part Two is subdivided into categories which cite reference books dealing with various subjects such as history, literature, and slavery. An addendum has also been added for material which has been recently announced for publication and not examined by this compiler.

Each item cited is numbered in sequential order beginning with 01. This numbering system is used to provide exact referrals from the author, title, and subject indices found at the back of the guide. A zero is used before each item number so that the user will not confuse them with page numbers when using the indices. Therefore, when a

number is cited in either of the three indices, it refers
to a specific reference book which can be found in sequential order within the guide.

The author, title, and subject indices will hope-
fully aid in using this guide and are considered to be an
integral part of it. The subject index attempts to offer
a more detailed topical approach to the items cited than is
possible through the basic organization of the guide
reflected in the table of contents. The subject indexing
has been based on the general nature of the item cited,
key words in the title, and unique aspects indicated in the
annotation. In using this guide it should be remembered
that, unless indicated otherwise, all terms used in the
subject index refer to black Americans.

As stated earlier, each title in this guide has been
identified by a number and these numbers are used for
indexing purposes. Throughout the subject index, those
numbers which have been underlined refer to reference books
dealing primarily with the topic being pursued; those
numbers not underlined refer to reference books which deal
with the subject under consideration but also contain substantial information of another nature. An example from
the subject index will illustrate this point.

Biographical sketches: <u>020</u>, 022, <u>023</u>, <u>024</u>, 027, 037

Although all of the numbers indicated under the preceding
subject heading refer to reference books which include

biographical sketches, only those numbers that are underlined are devoted exclusively to such sketches. The other
numbers listed identify books which contain biographical
sketches in addition to other information.

It is impossible to adequately thank everyone who has
been of assistance on this project, but some do deserve
special mention. I would like to thank my colleagues in
the Reference Department of Northwestern University Library,
and other members of the University Library staff, who have
generously extended their assistance, suggestions, encouragement, and patience during my compilation of this bibliographic guide. My special gratitude is also extended to
the Assistant University Librarian for Collection Development, Dr. Richard L. Press, for his unfailing aid and
encouragement in this project.

For typing early drafts of the manuscript I would also
like to thank Barbara Friel, Carol Kreider, and Alana
Milstein.

My special thanks are also extended to the members of
the Northwestern University Library Publications Committee
whose editorial assistance helped make this publication
possible. The members of this Committee are: Adele W. Combs,
Rolf H. Erickson (Chairman), R. Russell Maylone, Dorothy V.
Ramm, Don L. Roberts, and Peggy Steele.

Guy T. Westmoreland, Jr.

PART ONE

GENERAL REFERENCE SOURCES

Bibliographic Guides and Catalogs of

Special Library Collections

(01)

Bell and Howell/Atlanta University. Black Culture
    Collection. Cleveland, Bell and Howell, 1971.
    528 pp. on 101 leaves.

    Although the entries lack full bibliographic information,
this is a useful copy of the subject book catalog of Atlanta
University's Trevor Arnett Library, which includes both
African and Afro-American material. This collection is es-
pecially strong in material on American black culture since
1930. In addition, Bell & Howell microfilm price information is provided for various sections of the collection.

(02)

The Chicago Afro-American Union Analytic Catalog:
    An Index to Materials on the Afro-American in
    the Principal Libraries of Chicago. Boston,
    G.K. Hall, 1972. 5 vols.

    This published version of the catalog compiled by, and
housed at, the Chicago Public Library's George C. Hall
Branch, is a major resource tool for Afro-Americana. In
five volumes, the catalog includes over 75,000 entries of
Afro-American material held in five major Chicago libraries
(including the Hall Branch which specializes in Afro-
Americana) as of 1940.
    A wealth of annotated material in all published forms
(except newspapers) is organized by author, title, and
subject. Of special interest is the inclusion of analytics
of articles in over 1,000 foreign and domestic periodicals
published from the late 19th century to 1940.

(03)

<u>A Directory of Afro-Americana in Chicago Area</u>
<u>Libraries</u>. Chicago, The Newberry Library,
1971. 18 leaves.

A collection of statements made in 1970 by eight
Chicago area libraries, describing their respective collections in Afro-Americana and their related policies for
developing these collections.

(04)

Hampton Institute, Hampton, Va. <u>A Classified</u>
<u>Catalogue of the Negro Collection in the</u>
<u>Collis P. Huntington Library, Hampton</u>
<u>Institute</u>. Hampton, Va., Hampton Institute.
1940. 225 pp.

African folklore and black suffrage and politics are
among the wide range of social, cultural, economic, and
historical areas included in this subject catalog. The
catalog cites over five thousand titles on blacks in Africa
and America which were published during the 19th and early
20th centuries.

(05)

Hampton Institute, Hampton, Va., Collis P.
Huntington Memorial Library. <u>Dictionary</u>
<u>Catalog of the George Peabody Collection</u>
<u>of Negro Literature and History</u>. Westport,
Conn., Greenwood, 1972. 2 vols.

Whereas the 1940 catalog of this collection cited approximately 6,000 titles, this 1972 reproduction of the library's
card catalog cites most of the 15,000 items by and about
blacks throughout the world, now held in the Peabody Collection. Although the collection covers many subject areas
related to blacks, it is notably strong in American Civil War
History. Approximately 11,500 monographs covering many
subjects, in addition to more than 1,700 pamphlets and other
documents on slavery and the reconstruction period in the
U.S., are cited.
The catalog's dictionary arrangement provides access by
author, title, and subject entries, in one alphabetical
arrangement, to the collection's books, journals, newspapers, rare books, scrapbooks, slavery pamphlets, and
selected audiovisual material.

(06)

Heartman, Charles F. News Sheet of the Charles
    F. Heartman Collection of Material Relating
    to Negro Culture, Printed and in Manuscript.
    Hattiesburg, Miss., 1945. 7 nos. in 1 vol.

    Narratives, proceedings and minutes of various anti-
slavery organizations, and manuscripts, are among the areas
included in this collection of seven bibliographic news
sheets. They outlined the scope of bookseller Charles F.
Heartman's collection on black culture as of 1945.
                (See also: No. 015)

(07)

Historical Records Survey. District of
    Columbia. Calendar of the Writing of
    Frederick Douglass, in the Frederick
    Douglass Memorial Home, Anacostia, D.C.
    Washington, District of Columbia, His-
    torical Records Survey, 1940. 93 leaves.

    A selectively annotated catalog of 310 letters, speeches,
and other writings of Frederick Douglass. This collection
represents a large percentage of the writings of this major
19th century black American leader and demonstrates his
interest and participation in the abolition, temperance, and
women's suffrage movements in addition to the issues of
prison reform and labor rights. Cited, among many other
items, are letters written by Douglass to William Lloyd
Garrison, speeches before the American Anti-Slavery Society,
an address on the Dred Scott Decision, and a letter to
Benjamin Harrison.

(08)

Historical Records Survey. New York (City).
    Calendar of the Manuscripts in the
    Schomburg Collection of Negro Literature,
    Located at 135th Street Branch, New York
    Public Library. 1942. Reprint. New York,
    Andronicus, [1970?]. xviii, 548 pp.

    This descriptive bibliography of the manuscript collec-
tion in the noted Schomburg Collection also includes biographical sketches of many individuals mentioned in the
manuscripts.
    (See also: New York Public Library, Schomburg Collection
                No. 012)

4

(09)

Howard University, Washington, D.C. Library.
  Dictionary Catalog of the Arthur B.
  Spingarn Collection of Negro Authors.
  Boston, G.K. Hall, 1970. 2 vols.

A single alphabetical arrangement of author, title, and
subject entries, is used in this two volume catalog of
Howard University Library's Spingarn collection of material
written by blacks throughout the world. Highlights of the
material cited are very early Afro-American writing; slave
narratives and autobiographies, plus Caribbean, Afro-Cuban,
and Afro-Brazilian literature. Other features of this catalog are the analytical entries which provide citations to
hundreds of periodical articles and to authors included in
anthologies and similar publications. In addition, a section
on black composers and their music is appended to volume two.

(010)

Howard University, Washington, D.C. Library.
  Moorland Foundation. Dictionary Catalog
  of the Jesse E. Moorland Collection of
  Negro Life and History, Howard University,
  Washington, D.C. Boston, G.K. Hall, 1970.
  9 vols.

The Moorland collection of over 100,000 cataloged and
indexed items explores the whole realm of the black experience throughout the world. This nine volume catalog provides a single alphabetical approach by author, title, and
subject to this collection. Not only books and pamphlets,
but articles which appeared in monographic serials, periodicals, and some newspapers, are also cited.
    Volume one includes separate alphabetical and subject
arrangements of African and Afro-American periodicals held
in the collection, plus an index to biographies.

(011)

Negro History, 1553-1903; An Exhibition of Books,
  Prints, and Manuscripts From the Shelves of the
  Library Company of Philadelphia and the
  Historical Society of Pennsylvania...April
  17 to July 17, 1969. Philadelphia, [Library
  Company of Philadelphia], 1969. v, 83 pp.

A selective and descriptive listing of 16th to 19th century publications, dealing with black history, that are available in these two important collections.
                (Same title cited at No. 0140)

(012)

New York. Public Library. Schomburg Collec-
      tion of Negro Literature and History.
      <u>Dictionary Catalog of the Collection of</u>
      <u>Negro Literature and History</u>. Boston,
      G.K. Hall, 1962. 9 vols.

      A single alphabetical arrangement is used to provide
author, title, or subject approaches to the sources in this
important collection of material by and about black people
throughout the world. As of the publication date of the
basic nine volume catalog in 1962, the Schomburg collection
included over 36,000 bound volumes plus art objects, manuscripts, pamphlets, and other forms of material.
                  (See also: No. 08 and No. 013)

(013)

New York. Public Library. Schomburg Collection
      of Negro Literature and History.
      <u>Dictionary Catalog of the Schomburg</u>
      <u>Collection of Negro Literature and</u>
      <u>History</u>. Supplement I. Boston,
      G.K. Hall, 1967. 2 vols.

      The first supplement to the Schomburg Collection Catalog
includes approximately 7,000 new acquisitions plus several
hundred phonodiscs of America jazz, West Indian folk music,
and African music.

(014)

Race Relations Information Center. <u>Directory</u>
      <u>of Afro-American Resources</u>. Edited by Walter
      Schatz. New York, R.R. Bowker [1970]. xv,
      485 pp.

      A state-by-state descriptive record of primary source
material on the Afro-American, available in over 5,000
libraries, private agencies, civil rights and similar organizations. The entries are indexed by subject, individual,
location and institution.

(015)

Texas Southern University. Library. Heartman
      Negro Collection. <u>Catalogue: Heartman</u>
      <u>Negro Collection</u>. Houston, Texas Southern
      University Library, [1956], 325 pp.

      A variety of material including clippings, books,
periodicals, broadsides, and more, is included in this subject catalog of the approximately 15,000 items comprising
a major collection acquired from bookseller, Charles F.
Heartman. This collection explores the world-wide black
experience and is further described in Heartman's <u>News Sheet</u>
(No. 06).

Biographical Sources

(016)

Baskin, Wade. <u>Dictionary of Black Culture</u>.
New York. Philosophical Library, [1973].
493 pp.

Entries for individuals are emphasized in this historical and contemporary dictionary which also includes events, organizations, institutions, and publications of and/or about black America. Many of the entries, particularly those for individuals, lack adequate identification of dates and related information which would provide more definite historical identification.
(Same title cited at Numbers 031 and 0189)

(017)

Bell, Barbara L. <u>Black Biographical Sources</u>:
<u>An Annotated Bibliography</u>. New Haven; Yale
University Library, 1970. 20 pp.

A selected list of collective biographical sources for black Americans, emphasizing the period of 1860-1969.

(018)

Davis, Russell H. <u>Memorable Negroes in</u>
<u>Cleveland's Past</u>. Cleveland, Western
Reserve Historical Society, 1969. 58 pp.,
illus., maps, ports.

A collection of biographical sketches of 18 blacks who distinguished themselves in the history of Cleveland, Ohio from 1808 to 1968. Portraits for most of those individuals are included and accompany standard biographical information and narration of the impact on the life of Cleveland made by these black citizens.

(019)

Edmonds, Helen G. <u>Black Faces in High Places</u>:
<u>Negroes in Government</u>. New York, Harcourt,
Brace, Jovanovich. [1971]. vi, 277 pp.,
illus.

Short biographical sketches of American blacks who have held major political office in all branches and on all levels (local, state and federal) of government through 1970.

(020)

Metcalf, George R. <u>Up From Within: Today's</u>
<u>New Black Leaders</u>. New York, McGraw-Hill,
[1971]. xvi, 302 pp.

A compilation of eight extended biographical sketches of black Americans who typify what the author considers the third stage of the black revolution (i.e., blacks who are successfully competing in the wider U.S. society of economics and politics).

(021)

Negro Heritage. Reston, Va. Vol. 1-
    1961- . Monthly.

    Currently being published monthly, this pamphlet series
includes a large amount of biographical information and provides insight into black American heritage from both historical and current perspectives.

(022)

Ohio University, Athens. Center for Afro-
    American and Contemporary Issues. Athens,
    Ohio, Ohio University, Center for Afro-
    American Studies, 1972. 3 vols.

    This manual for college and university Black Studies
courses can also be used as an effective reference tool.
Part I is a guide to discussions of several contemporary
issues in Black Studies such as the black family and black
identity. Part II entitled "people Pieces," provides biographical profiles of 99 black Americans over the period of
1770 to 1971. Material written by and/or about the subject
of the profile is cited with each one. Part III includes
discussions of several historical topics, such as the New
York African Free School and black music, which are of
interest to Black Studies. These two topics are among many
which are graphically displayed on a fold-out historical
time line chart which outlines Afro-American history from
1770 to 1971. Two other time line charts are included which
outline the history of Afro-American authors and Afro-
American music respectively over the period of 1770 to 1971.
                (Same title cited at No. 0125)

(023)

Robinson, Wilhelmena S. Historical Negro
    Biographies. 2nd ed. International
    Library of Negro Life and History. New
    York, Publishers Co., [1968]. xii,
    291 pp., illus.

    A volume of the International Library of Negro Life and
History, this compilation explores the lives of over 500
black diplomats, authors, explorers, and many others from
all parts of the world, from the 14th to the late 20th
centuries.
                (Same title cited at No. 37i.)

(024)

Rogers, Joel A. <u>World's Great Men of Color</u>.
    Edited with an introduction, commentary,
    and new bibliography noted by John H.
    Clarke. [1946]. Reprint. New York,
    Macmillan, [1972]. 2 vols., illus., ports.

   This two volume collection of biographical profiles is
the result of over 50 years of research by the late black
historian and anthropologist Joel A. Rogers. Well researched,
these profiles generally average about seven or eight, and in
some cases, fifteen or more, pages per individual. Sources
of additional information are also cited with each profile
and in some cases a portrait of the individual is included.
   Volume I profiles 52 great men and women of African
descent who had a significant impact on the societies of
Asia and Africa from the period which preceded the birth of
Christ to the twentieth century. A few of those profiled
in Volume I are Aesop (c. 560 B.C.), Greek philosopher;
Nzingha or Ann Zingha (1582-1663), Queen of Matamba, West
Africa; Samuel Crowther (1806-1892), first African bishop
of the Anglican Church; and Haile Selassie I (1891-),
Emperor of Ethiopia.
   Volume II profiles 64 individuals of African descent
who had significant impact on Europe and the New World.
Two of those included from South America are Bernardino
Rivadavia (1780-1845), first president of the Argentine
Republic; and Carlos Gomes (1836-1896), Brazilian operatic
composer. Some of the great men of the West Indies profiled
are Toussaint L'Ouverture (1743-1803), Haitian revolutionary
leader; Alexander Petion (1770-1816), first president of
Haiti; and Ulises Heureaux (1845-1900), dictator of Santo
Domingo. Some of the blacks included from the United States
are Estevanico (d. 1540), explorer of the Southwest; Ira
Aldridge (1810?-1867), Shakespearean actor; Frederick
Douglass (1817-1895), founder of the newspaper <u>The North
Star</u> and dynamic advocate of emancipation and equality;
William Trotter (1872-1934), founder of the militant news-
paper <u>The Guardian</u>; Dr. Ernest Just (1883-1941), leading
biologist; and Henry Tanner (1859-1937), artist.

(025)

Spradling, Mary Mace. In Black and White:
    Afro-Americans in Print: A Guide to
    Afro-Americans Who Have Made Contribu-
    tions to the United States of America
    From 1619 to 1969. Kalamazoo, Mich.,
    Kalamazoo Library System, 1971.
    ix, 127 pp.

    Essentially a current and historical biographical index
citing notable black Americans with birth and/or death
dates; occupation, and specific sources for biographical
information on each individual. An index of individuals
by occupation is also included.

(026)

Swisher, Robert D.; Tullis, Carol; and Hicks,
    Richard, comps. Black American Biography,
    compiled by Robert Swisher/Black American
    Scientists, compiled by Carol Tullis/Black
    Americans in Public Affairs, compiled by
    Richard Hicks. Indiana University. Focus:
    Black America Bibliography Series.
    (Bloomington), Indiana University Libraries
    and Focus: Black America, Summer, 1969.
    52 pp.

    This compilation of three brief bibliographies is based
on the holdings of the Indiana University Libraries (as of
1969). The first title listed includes both collective
biographical works and those on individual black Americans
in many walks of life. The second provides bibliographic
material about black scientists in general; a list of black
scientists by subject (with sources indicated for biographical information on each); and books written by the scientists listed. Finally, a compilation of periodical and
monographic literature on individual black Americans in
public affairs is provided.

(027)

Toppin, Edgar A. A Biographical History of
    Blacks in America Since 1528. New York,
    McKay, [1971]. x, 499 pp.

    This narrative history which discusses many individuals
(black and white) and their role in the black American
historical experience also includes a biographical section
on 145 notable black Americans, spanning the historical
spectrum of blacks in America.

(028)

<u>Who's Who in Colored America; A Biographical</u>
<u>Dictionary of Notable Living Persons of</u>
<u>African Descent in America</u>. Vols. 1-6,
New York, Who's Who in Colored America
Corp., 1927-1941. Vol. 7, Yonkers-on-
Hudson, New York, Christian E. Burckel
& Associates, 1950. 7 vols., ports.

Seven editions were published in this series between
1927 and 1950 providing standard biographical information
on noted black Americans who were living at the time the
information was compiled for this publication. Many photographs also accompany these biographical sketches which
are largely devoted to prominent people in the various professions.

(029)

Williams, Ethel L. <u>Biographical Directory of</u>
<u>Negro Ministers</u>. New York, Scarecrow
Press, 1965. xi, 421 pp.

Biographical sketches providing basic information on
education, professional activities, addresses, etc. of
living black ministers.

(030)

Williams, Ethel. <u>Biographical Directory of</u>
<u>Negro Ministers</u>. 2nd ed. Metuchen,
New Jersey, Scarecrow Press, 1970. xii,
605 pp.

An updated and expanded version of the 1965 edition of
this title with the added feature of a geographical index of
the black ministers included.

Dictionaries, Encyclopedias, Handbooks

and Yearbooks

(031)

Baskin, Wade. Dictionary of Black Culture.
New York, Philosophical Library, [1973].
493 pp.

Entries for individuals are emphasized in this historical and contemporary dictionary which also includes events,
organizations, institutions, and publications of and/or
about black America. Many of the entries, particularly
those for individuals, lack adequate identification of
dates and related information which would provide more definite historical identification.
(Same title cited at numbers 016 and 0189)

(032)

Davis, John P. The American Negro Reference
    Book. Englewood Cliffs, N.J., Prentice-
Hall, [1966], xxii, 969 pp.

Scholarly articles ranging in subject matter from the
black urban family, to blacks in the fine arts, to a brief
survey of Afro-America history, constitute the major portion of this encyclopedic hand-book. Some of the many important statistical tables included cover population, employment, and economic conditions of American blacks.

(033)

Directory: National Black Organizations.
    Harlem, N.Y., Afram Associates, [1972].
    viii, 115 pp.

A directory of non-profit, black organizations whose
efforts in behalf of black people are on a national scale.
These organizations are listed alphabetically within eight
topical categories which include, among others, educational,
fraternal, and professional groups. Some of the facts provided for most of the organizations listed are the location
of their headquarters, names of key staff members and of-
ficers, lists of their publications, and lists of scholarships, awards and programs they sponsor. A brief state-
ment on the purpose or overall objective of each organization plus a list of its program activities and services,
is also provided.

(034)

Ebony. The Negro Handbook. comp. by the
    editors of Ebony. Chicago, Johnson,
    1966. 535 pp.

    Economic conditions, politics and professional activ-
ity are among the many areas covered in the statistical
and factual information presented in this dated, but still
useful, handbook on black America. A sampling of topics
covered includes black participation in U.S. wars; black
farms and farming; and a demographic analysis of the black
American population based on the 1960 census.

(035)

Encyclopedia of the Negro, Preparatory Vol-
    ume with Reference Lists and Reports,
    by W.E.B. DuBois...and Guy B. Johnson...
    and others. New York, The Phelps-
    Stokes Fund, 1945. 207 pp. Group port.

    The only volume which resulted from an ambitious pro-
ject (proposed by the Phelps-Stokes Fund in 1931) to pub-
lish a four volume Encyclopedia of the Negro using the
Encyclopedia of the Social Sciences as a model.

(036)

Haley, James T. Afro-American Encyclopedia;
    or the Thoughts, Doings, and Sayings of
    the Race. Nashville, Haley & Florida,
    1895. xiv, 639 pp. illus., ports.

    A 19th century sermon on the preferability of the term
"Afro-American' (or more precisely "Af-Merican") to that
of "Negro" in addition to a section of eulogies on the
death of Frederick Douglass are two examples of the many
interesting essays, sermons, speeches, etc., by black
Americans, included in this late 19th century encyclopedia.
    A wide variety of other material is also included such
as biographical profiles and photographs of many Afro-
Americans plus photographs and illustrations of their
schools, residences. churches, colleges, and hospitals.
    Black newspapers of that period are also listed and a
population breakdown of blacks and whites is provided for
each state and each county within the states.
    A chapter on black church history, a discussion of
slave songs, and a section of Afro-American poetry are
three more notable examples of material included.

International Library of Negro Life and
    History. New York, Publishers Co.,
    Under the auspices of the Associa-
    tion for the Study of Negro Life
    and History, 1967-1969. 10 vols.,
    illus., ports., facsims., tables.

Although each of the ten volumes published in this
series, International Library of Negro Life and History,
stand as separate bibliographic entities, together they
constitute an encyclopedia of the black experience primarily in the New World. Each of the ten volumes in the
series is well indexed, provides bibliographic references,
and makes abundant use of maps, illustrations, portraits,
etc.
    Three volumes by Charles Wesley (a,b,c) provide an
encyclopedic survey of black American history beginning
with the African background (a). This volume surveys the
first stage of Afro-American history from its African be-
ginnings to the slave trade, early Afro-American achievements, and early black abolitionists. Negro Americans in
the Civil War (b) continues the survey and explores slavery as an underlying issue of the war, the war itself and
emancipation, the aftermath of war, and the 13th, 14th, and
15th amendments to the U.S. Constitution. The Quest for
Equality...(c) brings the historical survey down to the
1960's. It explores, among other things, the roles of
black statesmen during reconstruction, the Harlem Renaissance, black soldiers in American wars, and the struggle
for equality in the 1950's and 60's.
    Black music and art (d) are surveyed in an anthology
of articles which cover the development of Afro-American
music from spirituals to minstrels, blues, jazz, and clas-
sical music. The development of art covers the heritage of
African art, blacks and modern art, recognition of black
artists' achievements, and today's contemporary artists.
    A collection of articles explores black American
achievements in the theatre (e), beginning with a study of
the African Company of Negro Actors in New York City in
1821. The black playwright is also explored and the
script of the first drama to appear on Broadway (1923),
written by a black (The Chip Woman's Fortune),is included.
The black actor, blacks in the dance, motion pictures, and
radio and television are also covered in this volume.
    Black literature (f) is introduced through a collection
of selections by various black authors and poets. Beginning with 18th century literature, selections are included
from such people as Briton Hammon, Gustavas Vassa and
Jupiter Hammon. This survey continues with representative
selections from the 19th century through the 20th century
and the 1960's.

Biographical information and photographs help tell the history of the black athlete (g) from the days of segregated sports to the black breakthrough into major league baseball by Jackie Robinson in 1946. Other milestones in the history of the black athlete bring this study to the contemporary issues of football, tennis, and golf.

Concentrating on the first three-fourths of the 20th century, the study on the history of blacks in medicine (h) explores the history of discrimination against black American patients and medical professionals and how this often combined with poverty caused an historical health gap between whites and blacks in the U.S. Early Afro-American healers during slavery and pre-civil war black physicians are also discussed.

Historical Negro Biographies (i) is a collection of biographical sketches of black Americans and is fully described in no. 023.

Documents which chronicle Afro-American history are collected in the volume entitled I Too Am America...(j). See no. 0141 for a fuller description of this title.

(a) Wesley, Charles H. In Freedom's Footsteps, From the African Background to the Civil War. International Library of Negro Life and History. New York, Publishers Co., [1968]. xii, 307 pp, illus., facsims., ports.

(b) Wesley, Charles H., and Patricia W. Romero, Negro Americans in the Civil War: From Slavery to Citizenship. (2nd ed. rev.)International Library of Negro Life and History. New York, Publishers Co.,[1969]. xi, 291 pp. illus., facsims., maps, plan, ports.

(c) Wesley, Charles H. The Quest for Equality: From Civil War to Civil Rights. International Library of Negro Life and History. New York, Publishers Co. [1968]. xii, 307 pp. illus., facsims., maps, plans, ports.

(d) Patterson, Lindsay, comp. Negro in Music and Art.International Library of Negro Life and History. New York, Publishers Co., [1967]. xvi, 304 pp. illus., ports.

(e)   Patterson, Lindsay, comp.
Anthology of the American Negro in the
Theatre: A Critical Approach. (2nd ed.)
International Library of Negro Life and
History. New York, Publishers Co., [1969].
xiv, 306 pp. illus., facsims., ports.

(f)   Patterson, Lindsay, comp. An
Introduction to Black Literature in
America, From 1746 to the Present.
International Library of Negro Life and
History. New York, Publishers Co., [1969] .
xvii, 302 pp. ports.

(g)   Henderson, Edwin B. and the editors
of Sport Magazine. The Black Athlete:
Emergence and Arrival. Introduction by
Jackie Robinson, International Library
of Negro Life and History. New York,
Publishers Co., [1969] . xiii, 306 pp.
illus.

(h)   Morais, Herbert M. The History of
the Negro in Medicine. (3rd ed.) International Library of Negro Life and History. New York, Publishers Co., [1969].
xix, 322 pp. illus.

(i)   Robinson, Wilhelmena S. Historical
Negro Biographies. (2nd ed.) International
Library of Negro Life and History. New
York, Publishers Co., [1968]. xii, 291 pp.
illus.

(j)   Romero, Patricia W., comp. I Too Am
America: Documents From 1619 to the Present. International Library of Negro Life
and History. New York, Publishers Co.,
[1968]. xv, 304 pp. illus., facsims., map.

(038)

International Library of Negro Life and
    History: Yearbook. New York, Pub-
    lishers Co., 1969- Annual.

    Providing a survey of recent developments in black
America, this is an annual supplement to the ten volume
International Library of Negro Life and History.

(039)

The Negro Handbook...1942-49. New York,
    W. Malliet and Company, 1942-49.
    Biennial.

    Covering such topics as business, religion, civil
rights, and the arts, the four editions of this biennial
handbook serve as a manual or almanac of current facts,
statistics, and general information on black America
for the period (1942-49).. somewhat similar in scope to
the Negro Yearbook, an Annual Encyclopedia of the Negro
...1912-1952.

(040)

Negro Year Book, An Annual Encyclopedia of
    the Negro. Tuskegee Institute. Ala.,
    Negro Year Book Pub. Co., 1912-1952.

    Eleven editions of this year book were published dur-
ing its forty year (1912-1952) life-span. It provides a
handbook approach to descriptive and statistical information on black historical and sociological issues.

(041)

Northrup, Henry D. The College of Life: Or
    Practical Self-Educator, A Manual of
    Self-Improvement for the Colored Race...
    1895. Reprint. Miami, Fla., Mnemosyne,
    1969. 656 pp., [80] pp. illus., ports.

    Originally published in 1895 as a self-educator for
Afro-Americans, this manual explored major aspects of 19th
century American culture (e.g. use of the English language;
etiquette; courtship and marriage; etc.) in the very pa-
tronizing and pedantic manner which was often customary
with that period. A descriptive survey of the first
thirty years of black progress after enancipation includes
useful biographical sketches of some early Afro- Americans.

(042)

Ploski, Harry A., and Roscoe C. Brown Jr.,
    comps. The Negro Almanac. New York,
    Bellwether, [1967]. xi, 1012 pp. illus.,
    maps, ports.

Beginning with a chronological historical review of the
Afro-American experience, this encyclopedic handbook also
explores monuments, landmarks, and documents of Afro-American history. The contemporary life of black America is
explored through a survey of civil rights organizations;
surveys of the economic, political, and social life of
black America with the abundant aid of statistical charts
and tables; plus a major historical and contemporary biographical section on blacks in various endeavors.
    A list of national Afro-American organizations plus an
historical and contemporary survey of Africa, are two more
major highlights of this well indexed title.

(043)

Ploski, Harry A., and Ernest Kaiser, comps.
    The Negro Almanac. 2nd ed. New York,
    Bellwether, [1971]. 1110 pp. illus.,
    maps, ports.

An updated and expanded version of this handbook, orig-
inally published in 1967 (no. 042), which reflects the
changes in contemporary black America and the overall role
of blacks in American society.

(044)

Rather, Ernest R., comp. Chicago Negro Alman-
    ac and Reference Book. Chicago, Chicago
    Negro Almanac Publishing Co., 1972
    viii, 256 pp., ports.

An historical and contemporary almanac of facts, figures,
and narrative on blacks in and from Chicago, including some
information on the overall national role of black Americans.
    Photographs of noted black, Chicago leaders are comple-
mented by a biographical section which provides a "who's
who" of blacks in Chicago.
    "Chicago Negro Firsts" is another notable section which
presents a chronology of profiles on important breakthrough
accomplishments by blacks throughout the history of Chicago.
    Also included are a variety of lists noting black
Chicagoans holding key governmental posts on all jurisdic-
tional levels and other similar accomplishments. An index
aids access to these lists as well as the other information included in the Almanac.

(045)

Rogers, Joel A. 100 Amazing Facts About the
    Negro, With Complete Proof: A Short Cut
    to the World History of the Negro. New
    York, Helga M. Rogers. Distributed by
    Sportshelf, New Rochelle, N.Y., c. 1957,
    1970 ed. 58 pp. illus., ports.

    The first part of this handbook lists 100 historical
facts about achievements and other aspects of the black experience throughout the world in a number of categories ranging from ancient civilization, science and invention, politics, to religion. The second part then cites, in numeri-
cal order, bibliographic sources to prove each of the 100
facts.

(046)

Wright, Richard R., comp. The Philadelphia
    Colored Directory: A Handbook of the
    Religious, Social, Political, Professional
    Business and Other Activities of the
    Negroes of Philadelphia. Philadelphia,
    Philadelphia Colored Directory Co., 1907.
    Reprint. Ann Arbor, Mich., Zerox Univ.
    Microfilms, n.d.

    This handbook of information on the 1907 black popula-
tion of Philadelphia provides a variety of information such
as population statistics; a list of blacks in various professions; a directory of churches by denomination with addresses, ministers' names, and membership figures; plus a
directory of black business firms. An extended list of
black property owners plus a list of books and pamphlets
by black Philadelphians are two other features included.

Indexes to Periodical Literature

(047)

Black Information Index. V. 1-   1970-   .
    Herndon, Va.; Infonetics, Inc. 1970-
    Bimonthly.

    Africa, black studies, book reviews, and politics are a
few of the areas covered in this topically arranged bi-
monthly index to current information by and about black
people. Periodicals, including many major black publications, form the basis of this index which also includes
references to monographs.

(048)

Chicago Public Library Omnibus Project...Subject
    Index to Literature on Negro Art Selected
    From the Union Catalog of Printed Mater-
    ials on the Negro in the Chicago Libraries.
    Chicago, Ill., Chicago Public Library
    Omnibus Project, 1941. 49 pp.

    Periodical literature is emphasized in this annotated
index, organized by subjects ranging from architecture and
art to sculpture and wood-carving.

(049)

A Guide to Negro Periodical Literature.
    V. 1-4, No. 3. Compiled by A.P. Marshall.
    Winston-Salem, N.C., A.P. Marshall. 1941-
    1946. Quarterly.

    This author/subject index to black periodical litera-
ture was published from 1941-1946.

(050)

Index to Periodical Articles By and About
 Negroes. V. 1- 1950- . Boston,
 G.K. Hall. 1950- Annual.

A decennial cumulation, Index to Selected Periodicals.
incorporates volumes one through ten (1950-1959) of this
index which was formerly entitled the Index to Selected
Negro Periodicals (from 1950-1954) and the Index to Selected Periodicals (from 1954-1960). With the title change in
1960, this became an annual publication compiled by the
staffs of the Hallie Q. Brown Memorial Library at Central
State University, Wilberforce, Ohio (the original compiler)
and the Schomburg Collection of the New York (City) Public
Library.
    Also, as of 1960, the index is divided into two parts:
part one is an index to periodicals received by the Hallie
Q. Brown Library and part two an index to articles on
black literature and history indexed by the Schomburg staff.

Multi-Subject Bibliographies

(051)

Baker, Augusta. <u>The Black Experience in
    Children's Books</u>. (New York) New
    York Public Library, 1971. iv, 109 pp.

Comprising the New York Public Library's James Weldon
Johnson Memorial Collection for children, this is a care-
fully selected comprehensive bibliography of children's
books which makes an honest assessment of the whole range
of the black experience in America and Africa.

(052)

California. San Fernando Valley State College,
    Los Angeles. Library. <u>The Black Exper-
    ience in the United States; A Bibliography
    Based on Collections of the San Fernando
    Valley College Library</u>. Northridge, Cali-
    fornia, San Fernando Valley State College
    Foundation, 1970. xiii, 162 pp. facsims.,
    ports.

A selective subject compilation of the library's
holdings on the black experience in the United States.

(053)

California. State College, Fresno. Library.
    <u>Afro- and Mexican-Americana: Books and
    Other Materials in the Library of Fresno
    State College Relating to the History,
    Culture, and Problems of Afro-Americans
    and Mexican-Americans</u>. Fresno, Calif.,
    Fresno State College. Library, 1969.
    109 pp.

Books plus federal and state government publications, in
addition to a brief list of masters theses and graduate
study papers, apparently completed at Fresno State College,
are included in this list. Although the Mexican-American
experience is explored in some of the citations included,
most of the titles cited deal with the Afro-American experience.
    Also included is a very brief list of periodicals, lack-
ing bibliographic or library holdings information. The major section of the list cites books in a topical arrangement without full bibliographic information for those
title cited.

(054)

California. State College, San Diego. Library.
   Afro-American Bibliography; List of the Books,
   Documents, and Periodicals on Black American
   Culture Located in San Diego State College
   Library. Compiled by Andrew Szabo. [San
   Diego], San Diego State College. Library.
   1970. 327 pp.

   Emphasizing comparatively current publications (1950-
1969), this topically arranged bibliography also includes
some representative titles of the 19th and early 20th centuries.

(055)

Davison, Ruth M. and April Legler, comps.
   Government Publications on the Negro in
   America, 1948-1968. Federal government
   publications comp. by Ruth M. Davison.
   State government publications comp. by
   April Legler. Indiana University. Focus:
   Black America Bibliography Series.
   Bloomington, Indiana University Libraries
   and Focus: Black America, Summer, 1969.
   29 pp.

   Listed by issuing agency (within each state for state
documents) the titles in this bibliography indicate the wide
range of material related to the black American experience
published by government agencies.

(056)

Du Bois, W.E.B., ed. A Select Bibliography
   of the Negro American. The Atlanta University Publications, no. 10. Atlanta,
   Atlanta Univ. Pr., 1905. 71 pp.

   A brief bibliography of bibliographies introduces this
selected listing of primarily 18th and 19th century titles
on black Americans which is arranged in two parts. Part
one, the larger of the two, lists pamphlets, books, government and private agency reports, and other material alphabetically by author. Part two lists periodical articles
organized by the title of the periodical. No subject approach to this bibliography is provided.

(057)

Ellis, Ethel M. Vaughan. The American Negro:
    A Selected Checklist of Books. Washington,
    Negro Collection, Howard University Library,
    1968, 46 pp.

    A short, topical reading list which also includes
periodicals, films and filmstrips.

(058)

Foreman, Paul B. and Mozell C. Hill. The Negro
    in the United States: A Bibliography. A
    Selected List of Reference and Minimum
    College Library Resources List. (Bulletin
    of the Oklahoma A. and M. College, V. 44,
    No. 5. February, 1947). Stillwater,
    Okla., 1947. 24 pp.

    A brief, general list of books, pamphlets and periodical
articles compiled by two sociologists in 1946.

(059)

Irwin, Leonard B., comp. Black Studies: A
    Bibliography. Brooklawn, N.J., McKinley,
    1973.

    A selective guide to the literature, published during
the last twenty years, of black American biography, history,
social conditions, and the African background.
    Designed as a bibliography for schools, libraries, and
the general reader, brief annotations are provided for most
of the titles listed and reading level interests (e.g.
adult, high school, etc.) are indicated for all titles included.

(060)

Kinton, Jack F. American Ethnic Groups: A
    Sourcebook. [3rd ed. Aurora, Illinois,
    Social Science and Sociological Resources,
    1973.] 173 pp.

    A bibliographic sourcebook for the study of American
ethnic groups citing both monographs and journal articles
and indicating which titles the compiler considers defini-
tive or of special merit. Cited in one section is material
on American Indians, Asian and European American ethnic
groups, and Spanish-speaking Americans.
    A separate section cites material on race relations and
African Americans, including, among other things, selected
books on race relations theory. Books on black history and
culture, schildren, family, protest and reform, and other
topics are also cited in this section.
    Lists of black and other ethnic American studies
centers, in addition to an evaluative list of films on
these ethnic groups, also highlight this study.

(061)

Krash, Ronald, et. al. Black America: A
    Research Bibliography. Rev. and enl. ed.
    Publication no. 6. St. Louis, Pius XII
    Library, St. Louis University, 1972.
    113 pp.

    A general, non-annotated list of the literature on
black America, arranged by subject categories and including
an author index. Whereas such standard categories as
history and biography are included in some comparatively
unique categories such as blacks-local studies, blacks-
state studies, and blacks-international studies are also
included. A selected list of government publications and
basic reference sources is also included.

(062)

Lewinson, Paul. A Guide to Documents in the
    National Archives: For Negro Studies.
    American Council of Learned Societies De-
    voted to Humanistic Studies. Committee
    on Negro Studies. Publications, no. 1.
    Washington, American Council of Learned
    Societies Devoted to Humanistic Studies,
    1947, x, 28 pp.

    A brief, annotated list organized by combined chrono-
logical and subject categories.

(063)

Miller, Elizabeth W., comp. The Negro in
   America: A Bibliography. Compiled
   for the American Academy of Arts and
   Sciences. Foreward by Thomas F. Pettigrew.
   Cambridge, Harvard University Press, 1966.
   xviii, 190 pp.

Both monographs and journal articles which were published primarily during the period between the Supreme Court
decision of Brown vs. Board of Education (May, 1954) and
the Voting Rights Act of 1965, are cited in this bibliography. The first major section is devoted to background
material, citing historical and demographic studies dealing
with black America in addition to biographies and autobiographies. One of the most extensive sub-sections covers
social institutions and social conditions, citing material
on topics such as the black family, religion, community
life, and the black press. Among other major topics
covered are intergroup relations, rural and urban problems,
and economics.

(064)

Miller, Elizabeth W., comp. The Negro in
   America: A Bibliography. 2nd ed. rev.
   and enl. Compiled by Mary L. Fisher.
   New Foreword by Thomas F. Pettigrew.
   Cambridge, Harvard University Press,
   1970. xx, 351 pp.

The second edition of this bibliography also concentrates on material, both monographs and journal articles,
published since 1954 but cites more studies published
before that date and extends the coverage to 1970. The
subject scope of this edition has also been expanded including new sections on the arts; folklore and literature,
including literary criticism; and music. More extensive
coverage has also been given to Afro-American history and
social institutions, and to economic, educational, and
political issues in the American black community. An
expanded guide to further research is another feature
of this edition.

(065)

National Urban League. Dept. of Research.
   Selected Bibliography on the Negro. 3rd
   ed. November, 1940. New York, National
   Urban League. Dept. of Research, 1940. 58 pp.

A general, annotated bibliography arranged by subject
categories.

(066)

National Urban League. Dept. of Research.
    Selected Bibliography on the Negro.
    4th ed. June, 1951. New York,
    National Urban League. Dept. of Re-
    search, 1951. 124 pp.

    An updated version of the National Urban League's 1940
publication of the same title.

(067)

National Urban League. Dept. of Research.
    Source Materials on the Urban Negro in the
    United States: 1910-1937, A List of Se-
    lected Data Prepared by the National
    Urban League and Its Affiliated Branches.
    New York, National Urban League. Dept. of
    Research, 1937. 36 pp.

    Including, among others, community surveys and surveys
of labor conditions, this is a selected bibliography of re-
sults attained from investigations by the Urban League, and
other organizations, into the condition of urban American
blacks from 1910-1937.

(068)

The Negro; A List of Significant Books. 8th ed. New York,
    New York Public Library, 1960. 25 pp.

    A brief, annotated subject list based on the holdings
of the Countee Cullen Branch of the New York Public Library.

(069)

The Negro in Print. v. 1, no. 1- , May 1965-   .
    Washington, Negro Bibliographic and Re-
    search Center, 1965-   . Bimonthly.

    Also known as Bibliographic Survey: The Negro in Print,
this annotated, periodically issued, bibliography of current monographs is now published every other month except
July. Its basic format is by literary style (e.g. fiction,
non-fiction, and poetry) but some recent issues have included citations to pamphlets, periodical articles, and books
on special subject areas (e.g. Black English).

(070)

New Jersey Library Association. Bibliography
    Committee. New Jersey and the Negro: A
    Bibliography, 1715-1966. Trenton, 1967.
    196 pp.

    This bibliography was conceived as an aid to the stim-
ulation of research on the Afro-American in New Jersey.
Including material in many published and unpublished forms,
it covers the lives of blacks in New Jersey, the role of
the state in the history of black Americans, and attitudes
of whites in New Jersey toward blacks.

(071)

New York (City). City University of New
    York. New York City Community College.
    Library. Black Perspectives: A Bibli-
    ography. New York, Library Department,
    New York City Community College, The City
    University of New York, [1971]. 68 pp.

    Political, socio-economic, and cultural experiences of
blacks in North America, the Caribbean, and Africa are explored in this survey of the holdings of the New York City
Community College Library. Monographs on the Afro-American
and African experiences are organized in the two primary
sections of this bibliography using categories such as
biography, education, and religion. A briefer section
cites monographs on the experience of blacks in the Caribbean.

(072)

New York (City) Public Library. No Crystal
    Stair; A Bibliography of Black Literature.
    New York, New York Public Library, 1971.

    A selected, annotated list of significant books pub-
lished since 1965, in addition to selected classic titles
from earlier years, in various subject areas of Afro-
Americana (e.g. history, politics, literature, etc.)

(073)

Porter, Dorothy B., comp. The Negro in the
    United States; A Selected Bibliography.
    Library of Congress. Washington, Gov't.
    Print. Off., 1970. x, 313 pp.

    Emphasizing recently published monographs, this exten-
sive bibliography, based on the holdings of the Library of
Congress, is arranged by broad subject categories. The
author-subject index provides a more detailed approach than
the author's Working Bibliography on the Negro in the
United States.

(074)

Porter, Dorothy B., comp. A Working Bibli-
    ography on the Negro in the United
    States. [Ann Arbor, Mich.?], Xerox
    University Microfilms, 1969.

    This subject bibliography includes prices for many
titles cited and was compiled as a working guide for libraries involved in developing collections of Afro-
Americana. Although this title is briefer than the compiler's 1970 publication: The Negro in the United States:
A Selected Bibliography (No. 073), it includes many titles
not found in the later publication. Also included is a
brief list of Afro-American periodicals.

(075)

Prince George's County Memorial Library.
    Oxon Hill Branch. Reference Dept.
    Selective List of Government Publica-
    tions About the American Negro. Pre-
    pared for Negro History Week, February,
    1969. [Hyattsville, Md.], Prince
    George's County Memorial Library, [1969?].
    26 pp.

    A brief, selectively annotated, list of recent free or
inexpensive federal government publications about American
blacks. Lacking both a table of contents and an index. the
publications are listed by issuing agency and include
price information. Being a list of recent publications,
nothing is listed which was published prior to 1967.

(076)

Prince George's County Memorial Library.
    Oxon Hill Branch.   Reference Dept.
    Selective List of Government Publications
    About the American Negro. (Hyattsville,
    Md.), Prince George's County Memorial
    Library, [1970?].   50 pp.

    An expanded and updated version of this title with
basically the same characteristics as the 1969 edition
discussed above.   However, in this edition no publications
are listed which were published prior to 1968 nor are any
listed which have appeared in earlier editions of this
title.

(077)

Professional Guide to the Afro-American In
    Print: A Bibliography of Current Works
    By and About the Black Man of America.
    Compiled by Gladys M. Sturges.   Nor-
    mandy, Mo.   1969-   .   Semiannual.

    A selectively annotated, alphabetical list of 450
general monographic titles on the contemporary and historical experiences of Afro-Americans.   Also included in the
first edition is a descriptive list of current African
literature.

(078)

Ross, Franklin A.   A Bibliography of Negro
    Migration.   1934.   Reprint.   New York,
    B. Franklin, [1969].   251 pp.

    1200 titles (which appeared from 1865 to 1932), in a
variety of published an unpublished forms, are included
in this report of a 1934 annotated compilation covering the
migration of Afro-Americans from rural to urban areas and
from the South to the North from 1865 to 1932.   The material
included is also classified in separate sections by geographical and topical categories.

(079)

Tennessee.   Dept. of Education.   Division of
    School Libraries.   The Negro; A Selected
    List for School Libraries of Books By or
    About the Negro in Africa and America.
    Nashville, Tenn., State Dept. of Educa-
    tion, 1941.   48 pp. illus.

    An example of a selected, annotated, and topical list
of what were described as the best books on Afro-Americana
for elementary and high school students in 1941.

(080)

Treworgy, Mildred L. <u>Negroes in the United</u>
<u>States; A Bibliography of Materials for</u>
<u>Schools, Approvable for Purchase in</u>
<u>Pennsylvania Under NDEA Provisions. With</u>
<u>a Supplement of Recent Materials on Other</u>
<u>Minority Peoples</u>. University Park, Pa.
(Available from the Office of the Direc-
tory of Libraries, Pennsylvania State
University). 1967. ix, 93 pp.

Emphasizes current titles of instructional value for
secondary education in addition to a small list for primary education.

(081)

U.S. Air Forces in Europe. <u>A Bibliography</u>
<u>on the Black American</u>. USAFE Pamphlet
212-3. Prepared by USAFE Library, FL 5600,
Lindsey Air Station, West Germany and Base
Library, FL 5604, Wiesbaden Air Base, West
Germany. APO New York 09633, Department
of the Air Force Headquarters, U.S. Air
Forces in Europe.

Annotations from various reviewing media are included
for many of the titles listed in this general, multi-
subject bibliography. Some of the sections of note include
a rather extensive one on biography and personal narrative
and others on literature and music. In addition, there is
an extensive section on audiovisual materials including
cassettes, phonograph records, motion pictures, and filmstrips.

(082)

U.S. Library of Congress. Division of Bibliography. <u>Select List of References on</u>
<u>the Negro Question</u>. Compiled under the
direction of Appleton Prentiss Clark
Griffin. 2nd issue, with additions.
Washington, Govt. Print. Off., 1906.
61 pp.

Books (many with content information cited) and periodical articles from the 18th century to 1906 are included in this unclassified list dealing with black Americans.

(083)

Walters, Mary D. Afro-Americana: A Comprehensive Bibliography of Resource Materials
in the Ohio State University Libraries By
or About Black Americans. Columbus, Office
of Education Services, Ohio State University Libraries, 1969. 220 pp.

Over 3000 titles are cited in this multi-subject bibliography which lists books in the Ohio State University
Libraries, of significance to the study of Afr-Americans.
Author and title indexes are included and categories such
as religion, slavery, and music are used in the organization of the bibliography.

(084)

Welsch, Erwin K. The Negro in the United
States; A Research Guide. Bloomington,
Indiana University Press, 1965. xiii,
142 pp.

A guide to significant books, periodicals, and essays
to be used in various subject categories (e.g. history
and the arts) of research on black Americans.

(085)

West, Earle H., comp. A Bibliography of
Doctoral Research on the Negro, 1933-1966.
[Ann Arbor Mich.,] University Microfilms,
1969. vii, 134 pp.

Social institutions, economic status, and history are
three of the seven broad categories used to organize over
1400 dissertation titles accepted by American universities
from 1933 to 1966, covering all aspects of the Afro-
American experience and race problems in the U.S. Many of
the dissertations included are available from xerox University Microfilms (Ann Arbor, Mich.) and these are accom-
panied by a short annotation and the University Microfilms
order number.

(086)

West, Earle H., comp. A Bibliography of Doctoral
Research on the Negro. Supplement, 1967-1969.
[Ann Arbor, Mich., Xerox University Microfilms]
n.d. 26 pp.

As with the original edition of this bibliography, the
supplement cites dissertations which cover the full range
of experiences of black Americans. The supplement provides expanded coverage by citing dissertations accepted
by American universities from 1967 through 1969.

(087)

Williams, Daniel T. Eight Negro Bibliographies.
    New York, Kraus Reprint, 1970. 1 vol.
    (various pagings) illus.

    Included in this compilation are selective bibliographies
on the Southern students' protest movement through the sit-
ins of 1960; the Southern freedom rides (1961); James Meredith and the University of Mississippi; Black Muslims in
the U.S.; Martin Luther King, Jr.; Booker T. Washington;
lynching in America (plus statistics from the lynching records for 1882 to 1968 at Tuskegee Institute); and finally
Marcus Garvey (with selected copies of his correspondence).

(088)

Work, Monroe N. A Bibliography of the Negro
    in Africa and America. New York, H.W. Wilson,
    1928. Reprint. New York, Octagon Books,
    1970. xxi, 698 pp.

    A major bibliographic compilation citing over 17,000
books, pamphlets, and periodical articles, in various langu-
ages, which the introduction describes as the most significant material published prior to 1928 on the black experience in Africa and America. The bibliography is divided
into two major parts with part one dealing with blacks in
Africa and part two blacks in America. These two parts
are sub-divided into a total of 74 chapters covering a wide
variety of topics. A few of the topics included are African
civilizations and African laws and customs (covered in part
one), blacks and the discovery of America, slave insurrec-
tions, education of Afro-Americans, and black suffrage
(covered in part two). Part two also includes a separate
section exploring the artistic, political, racial, and
other contemporary (c. 1928) experiences of blacks in the
West Indies and Latin America.

PART TWO

SUBJECT AREA REFERENCE SOURCES

Civil Rights and Black America

(089)

Adams, A. John. Civil Rights; A Current Guide
    to the People, Organizations, and Events.
    New York, Bowker, 1970. viii, 194 pp.

    A combined list providing biographical information on
individuals and descriptions of organizations prominent
during the civil rights movement from 1945 to 1970. Two of
the appendices included are a chronology of civil rights
from 1954 to 1970 and the voting records of congressmen on
civil rights legislation from 1960 to 1968.

(090)

American Civil Liberties Union. American Civil
    Liberties Union Papers: A Guide to the Records
    of the A.C.L.U. Cases 1912-1946. Stony
    Brook, N.Y., Archives of Social History, 1971.
    iii, 87ℓ.

    A list of the material compiled by the A.C.L.U. dealing
with many of the civil liberties issues it had an interest
in from 1912 to 1946, including the Scottsboro cases. The
extensive A.C.L.U. collection includes newspaper clippings,
court briefs, letters, reports, and other material dealing
with civil liberties. This list is not an index to these
papers but rather a sequential volume list which follows
the chronological period to 1912 to 1946. Each volume is
identified by very broad categories such as correspondence
or clippings from various states.

(091)

Barker, Lucius J. and Twiley W. Barker, Jr.
    Civil Liberties and the Constitution;
    Cases and Commentaries. Englewood Cliffs,
    N.J., Prentice-Hall, 1970. vii, 471 pp.

    This general survey of civil liberties in the United
States includes a chapter on the constitutional standards
of equality and black Americans. A brief historical introduction precedes a discussion of case law pertinent to the
constitutional issues involved in the black American's
search for equal rights. Issues such as public education,
transportation, and voting rights are explored in this con-
text. The decisions on twelve U.S. Supreme Court cases,
dealing with equal rights and black Americans, are also included.

(092)

Brooks, Alexander D. Civil Rights and Liber-
    ties in the United States, An Annotated
    Bibliography. With a Selected List of
    Fiction and Audiovisual Materials Collect-
    ed by Albert A. Alexander and Virginia H.
    Ellison. New York, Civil Liberties Educa-
    tional Foundation, 1962. 151 pp.

    A descriptive list of audiovisual materials is also in-
cluded in this annotated bibliography of monographs which
is now somewhat dated. This historical and contemporary
bibliographic survey of civil liberties includes a section
on intergroup relations which deals most directly with
blacks and civil rights. This section explores such topics
as the nature of prejudice, legal aspects of civil rights,
and discrimination.

(093)

Friedman, Leon, Comp. The Civil Rights Reader;
    Basic Documents of the Civil Rights Move-
    ment. New York, Walker, 1968. xx, 382 pp.

    A compilation of such milestone documents as: The Re-
port of the President's Committee on Civil Rights (1947);
Brown vs. Board of Education of Topeka (1954); "I Have A
Dream" (speech by Martin Luther King, Jr.---1963); "Free-
dom--When?", by James Farmer (1965); and the civil rights
acts of 1957, 1960, and 1964.

(094)

Sobel, Lester A., ed. Civil Rights, 1960-66.
    New York, Facts on File, [1967] xii, 504 pp.

    A detailed table of contents and a very detailed index
aid the reference value of this chronology of summaries
which survey the black American struggle for civil and hu-
man rights from 1960 through 1966.
    Events, legislation, locations, people, etc. are dis-
cussed as they applied to such issues as the sit-ins, freedom rides, voting rights struggle, and school desegregation.
Some of the other issues surveyed are the Civil Rights Acts
of 1960 and 1964, the Voting Rights Act of 1965, and the
"Black Power" movement.

(095)

Tuskegee Institute. Dept. of Records and
    Research. Civil Rights and the Negro:
    A List of References Relating to Present
    Day Discussions. Comp. by Jessie P. Guz-
    man. Tuskegee Institute, Ala. 1950.

    Education, employment, and the law are three of the
categories covered in this historical look at the civil rights
of black Americans.

Drama, Fine Arts, Music, and Sports

(096)

Cederholm, Theresa D. Afro-American Artists:
    A Bio-Bibliographical Directory. Boston,
    Boston Public Library, 1973, 348 pp.

    Both historical and contemporary black American craftsmen,
painters, photographers, sculptors, and other artists, are
alphabetically listed in this directory which provides standard biographical information such as date of birth and
education.
    Additional information provided includes: titles and
exhibitions of the artists' works, awards received, and
collections where their work is displayed.
    An extensive bibliography lists sources of additional
information about each artist profiled and about black
artists in general.

(097)

Chilton, John. Who's Who of Jazz! Storyville
    To Swing Street. Foreword by Johnny Simmen.
    Philadelphia, Chilton, [1972]. 419 pp., ports.

    Many well-known, and not so well-known, black musicians
are included in this compilation of biographical profiles
of over 1,000 American jazz musicians born before 1920.
    These profiles outline the artists' careers including
such information as place and date of birth, locations and
dates of selected performances, and membership in various
performing groups. Numerous photographs of individual
black jazz artists and of black jazz groups are also
included.

(098)

Feather, Leonard G. The Encyclopedia of Jazz.
    New ed., rev., enl. and brought up-to-date.
    Appreciations by Duke Ellington, Benny
    Goodman, and John Hammond. New York,
    Horizon Press, 1960. 527 pp., illus.,
    (music), ports.

    An historical survey of jazz and a chapter on the
nature of jazz are two highlights of this encyclopedia
which is an expanded and enlarged version of the first
edition (1955). This new edition includes new material and
incorporates the contents of the first edition and the two
yearbooks which followed: i.e., The Encyclopedia Yearbook
of Jazz (1956) and The New Yearbook of Jazz (1958).
    Most of the encyclopedia is devoted to biographical
sketches of over 2,000 jazz musicians including many photographs of black jazz artists, both individual performers
and groups. Black influence in jazz is demonstrated through
the inclusion of many early blues singers in these sketches
in addition to the other black jazz artists. Information
provided for each artist covers his background and career
in addition to a selected discography. Long sketches are
generally provided for major jazz figures.

(099)

Feather, Leonard G. The Encyclopedia of Jazz
    in the Sixties. Foreword by John Lewis.
    New York, Horizon Press, 1966. 312 pp.,
    plates, ports.

    Includes an examination of the directions jazz took
during the 1960's and the personalities involved. As in
the earlier editions of this title, biographical sketches
of jazz musicians make up the major portion of this
encyclopedia. This edition includes musicians who were
prominent prior to the 1960's but were still very active
in the jazz world of the 60's in addition to new major
jazz artists of the 1960's.

(0100)

Gold, Robert S. A Jazz Lexicon. New York,
    Knopf, 1964. xxvi, 363 pp.

    The author of this dictionary explains that the langu-
age or slang of the jazz world, herein defined, resulted
from a fusion of the language of the general black popu-
lace and of jazz musicians. Many of the terms included
have now lost their exclusiveness as jazz terms and have
been adopted by the general public, black and/or white,
as slang. Each term is identified as to its use as a part
of speech, its etymological derivation, and its definition.
In addition, examples, including dates, are included which
cite the term's use or further definition by individuals,
newspaper or journal articles, etc.

(0101)

Hatch, James V. Black Image On the American
    Stage; A Bibliography of Plays and Musicals,
    1770-1970. New York, DBS Publications,
    [1970]. xiii, 162 pp.

    Plays written by black playwrights, or based on a
black theme, or containing at least one black character,
make up this list of works which displayed the black image
on the American stage.

(0102)

Irvine, Betty Jo and McCabe, Jane A., comps.
    Fine Arts and the Black American, compiled
    by Betty Jo Irvine/Music and the Black
    American, compiled by Jane A. McCabe.
    Indiana University. Focus: Black America
    Bibliography Series. Bloomington , Indiana
    University Libraries and Focus Black America,
    Summer, 1969. 33 pp.

    Emphasizing material published in the last twenty years,
both of the bibliographies in this compilation are based on
the monographic holdings of the Indiana University Libraries. The first compilation includes a list of black artists, general books about black art and artists, plus a
few on individual artists. General subject categories
such as jazz music and musicians, spirituals, and minstrels are used to organize the material in the second compilation which deals with music and the black American.

(0103)

Lawson, Hilda J. The Negro in American Drama
    (Bibliography of Contemporary Negro Drama).
    Urbana, Ill., 1939. 13 pp.

    A short, selected, and descriptive author list (indica-
ting black authorship where applicable) of published black
plays of the early 20th century.

(0104)

McCabe, Jane A.; Wood, Robert S. and Wilmer H.
    Baatz, comps. Black Entertainers and the
    Entertainment Industry, compiled by Jane
    McCabe/Black American Athletes, compiled
    by Robert S. Wood and Wilmer H. Baatz.
    Indiana University. Focus: Black America
    and Focus: Black America, Summer, 1969.
    23 pp.

    Both selective bibliographies in this compilation ex-
plore their subject interests (i.e. black entertainers, etc.
and black American athletes) in a general manner (emphasizing periodical literature and monographs published since
1948) with a few biographical citations.

(0105)

Merriam, Alan P. A Bibliography of Jazz.
    With the assistance of Robert J. Brenford.
    [Publications of the American Folklore Society.
    Bibliographical Series, v. 4, 1954.] Philadel-
    phia, American Folklore Society, 1954. Re-
    print, New York, Kraus, 1970. xiii, 145 pp.

    This bibliography is useful in illustrating the black
American experience as it has related to the development of
jazz music.
    Over 3,000 entries are cited alphabetically by author
listing books, newspaper and periodical articles, pamphlets,
and other material dealing with many aspects of jazz and
jazz musicians. The major emphasis of each title is indicated by one or more of 32 different codes such as
"(J & D)," meaning jazz and the dance, or "(Rev)," meaning
book review. Also listed are over 100 magazines which
have been completely or primarily devoted to jazz.
    Through the subject index, biographical, critical, and
other studies on jazz musicians can be identified. A few
of the black artists cited are: Louis Armstrong, Duke
Ellington, W.C. Handy, Billie Holiday, Joseph (King)
Oliver, Bessie Smith, and Thomas (Fats) Waller.

Economic Life and Business Affairs

(0106)

Michalak, Thomas J., comp. Economic Status
and Conditions of the Negro. Indiana
University. Focus: Black America Bibli-
ography Series. Bloomington, Indiana
University Libraries and Focus: Black
America, Summer, 1969. 21 pp.

Discrimination in employment and manpower training are
among the topics covered in this selective bibliography.

(0107)

National Minority Business Directories, Inc.
National Black Business Directory 1971.
[Minneapolis, National Buy-Black Campaign,
1970.] 60 pp. ports.

A national directory of profit-making firms which are
at least 50% black owned and deal on a nationwide scope.
This title has now been superseded by the National Minority
Business Directory.

(0108)

National Minority Business Directory. 1972.
Minneapolis, National Minority Business
Campaign, 1971. ports.

Listing over 1600 firms owned by all minority groups in
the United States, this annual directory supersedes the
National Black Business Directory (no. 0107) and includes
Standard Industrial Classification numbers for the various
business categories which incorporate the listed firms.

(0109)

U.S. Bureau of Apprenticeship and Training.
Directory for Reaching Minority Groups.
Washington, Govt. Print. Off., 1970.
255 pp.

A national list by state and city of individuals and
organizations who have access to minority groups for purposes of explaining to them the various affirmative action
programs in job training and job opportunities that are
available.

(0110)

U.S. Bureau of Foreign and Domestic Commerce
(Dept. of Commerce)...The Negro in Business--
1936; A Bibliography, Prep. by the Negro
Affairs Division. Washington, 1936. 13 pp.

Education

(0111)

A Chance To Go To College: A Directory of
    800 Colleges That Have Special Help for
    Students from Minorities and Low Income
    Families. New York, College Entrance
    Examination Board, 1971. A-46. pp.,
    246 pp.

Descriptive information on 829 American colleges and
universities which offer special help or programs for minority students or those from low income families. Admission
requirements, fees and tuition, and special programs available, are included in the information provided for each
institution.

(0112)

Bengelsdorf, Winnie. Ethnic Studies in Higher
    Education: State of the Art and Biblio-
    graphy. Assisted by Susan Norwitch and
    Louis Vrande. Washington, D.C., American
    Association of State Colleges and Uni-
    versities, 1972. 260 pp.

A general "state of the art" review of ethnic studies
in higher education precedes bibliographic surveys on
ethnic studies of the following groups: Asian-Americans,
blacks, Chicanos, Indians of America, Puerto Ricans and
other Spanish-speaking Americans, and white ethnics. Sections
on multi-ethnic studies and teacher training have also been
included.
    As with the other sections, the one on Black Studies
cites both periodical and monographic titles and most of
these are annotated. Included in this section are references to surveys and research studies, pending research,
general information, and history and sociology sources.
Another feature of this study is a state-by-state list of
institutions offering Black Studies courses and/or programs.

(0113)

Egerton, John. State Universities and Black
    Americans: An Inquiry Into Desegregation
    and Equity for Negroes in 100 Public
    Universities, Atlanta, Southern Education
    Foundation, 1969. 96 pp. illus., tables.

    Black and overall total student enrollment statistics
are presented in this 1968 survey of the 100 member institutions of the National Association of State Universities
and Land-Grant Colleges. Ninety-seven of the institutions
reported statistics and these are cited in the following
categories: 17 formerly all black institutions in Southern
and border states, 28 formerly all white institutions from
the same geographical area, 11 Eastern institutions, 15
Midwestern, and 26 Western institutions. Detailed narrative studies on the education of blacks are included for 5
of these 97 institutions.

(0114)

Fichter, Joseph H. Graduates of Predominantly
    Negro Colleges: Class of 1964. U.S. Public
    Health Service Pub., no 1571. Washington,
    Govt. Print. Off., [1967]. xix, 262 pp.

    This statistical study conducted by the National Opin-
ion Research Center and cosponsored by the U.S. Dept. of
Labor and the National Science Foundation, is a socio-
economic survey of a representative sample of blacks who
graduated from predominantly black colleges in 1964.
    Inclusion of a subject index would aid the use of this
survey as a reference book. However, an extensive list
of the volume's statistical tables, topical chapters, and
the statistics themselves, aid the reference value of the
study. Among other chapter topics are childhood experiences of these graduates, black female graduates, employment plans, plus the issue of race and job opportunities.

(0115)

Fichter, Joseph H. Negro Women Bachelors:
    A Comparative Exploration of the Exper-
    iences and Expectations of College Grad-
    uates of the Class of June, 1961.
    Chicago, National Opinion Research Center,
    1965. xii, 154 pp. tables.

The author's 1961 survey, Young Negro Talent...(no.0116),
combines male and female students in its statistical comparisons of blacks and whites graduating from college in
the spring of 1961. The first seventy tables of this study
(Negro Women Bachelors...)makes the same black-white
statistical comparisons as the aforementioned title but for
females only. Both studies cover a wide range of educational, sociological, and psychological topics.
The second section of this title, tables 71-118, covers
statistics obtained in a survey taken one year after the
graduation (spring, 1962) of the class of 1961. This survey covers such things as marital status, various aspects
of graduate school attendance, and various aspects of jobs
held by these graduates.
The last section, tables 119-135, surveys the class of
1961 two years after graduation. These last two sections,
tables 71-135, include comparisons between males and females.

(0116)

Fichter, Joseph H. Young Negro Talent; Survey
    of the Experiences and Expectations of
    Negro Americans Who Graduated From College
    in 1961. Chicago, National Opinion Re-
    search Center, 1964. vi. 63 pp.

A variety of tabular information is supplemented by text
on such major topics as educational attainment of parents;
reactions to various academic courses; plans for graduate
study; and reactions to various professions, in this comparative study of black and white college graduates.

(0117)

Graduate and Professional School Opportunities
    for Minority Students. 3rd ed. Princeton,
    N.J., Educational Testing Service, [1971.]
    240 pp.

A survey of graduate and professional programs at various institutions which provides general information on
available financial aid, minority enrollment figures, and
other useful information for minority applicants.

(0118)

Intensive Summer Studies Program. <u>Graduate
Study Opportunities For Minority Group
Students</u>. 2nd ed. (n.p.) Harvard-Yale-
Columbia Intensive Summer Studies Pro-
gram, [Introd. 1970]. 179 pp.

An outline of basic information (e.g. person to contact,
minority enrollment, special comments, etc.) on graduate
school opportunities for minority students, organized by
schools or departments for the institutions listed.

(0119)

Jay, James M. <u>Negroes in Science: Natural
Science Doctorates, 1876-1969</u>. Detroit,
Belamp Pub., [1971]. ix, 87 pp.

A statistical study based upon data collected on 587,
out of an estimated total of 650, black Americans who received doctoral degrees in the natural sciences between
1876 and 1969. Two of the topics explored are the origins
of the degree recipients by geographical location and under-
graduate institution. Another point of interest is the
special section on black female recipients of doctoral
degrees in the natural sciences.

(0120)

Johnson, Harry A. <u>Multimedia Materials for
Afro-American Studies; a Curriculum
Orientation and Annotated Bibliography
of Resources</u>. New York, R.R. Bowker,
1971. 353 pp.

Major position papers on black studies programs, and
other aspects of black education, lead off this annotated
bibliography of audiovisual material geared to aiding the
teaching of black studies courses.

(0121)

Koblitz, Minnie W. <u>The Negro in Schoolroom
Literature; Resource Materials for the
Teacher of Kindergarten Through the Sixth
Grade.</u> [New York Center for Urban Educa-
tion, 1967.] iii, 67 pp.

This critically annotated bibliography (also indicating reading age for the titles included) in such areas as
general biography, black history, etc., is geared to
material which will aid children in the appreciation of
the heritage of black Americans.

(0122)

McCabe, Jane A. Education and the Afro-American.
    Indiana University. Focus: Black America
    Bibliography Series. Bloomington, Indiana
    University Libraries and Focus: Black
    America, 1969.

(0123)

National Alliance of Businessmen. Directory
    of Predominantly Black Colleges and Uni-
    versities in the United States of America.
    Washington, National Alliance of Business-
    men, [1972?]. 91 pp.

   Although geared to the business community as a source
of information for a program of aid to minority colleges
and universities, this is a useful directory for others
seeking information on black institutions of higher education. An alphabetical guide to 85 predominantly black
colleges and universities, this directory includes names
of key administrators, enrollment figures, and the types
of degrees offered by each institution. The number of
degrees granted during recent years, by each institution,
plus a brief description of each institution and a list
of its organizational affiliations, is also provided.

(0124)

National Scholarship Service for Negro Students.
    Research Reports. v. 1-   Jan. 1972-   .
    Minneapolis, Survey Research Services,
    National Computer Systems, 1972.

   This first study in this series is entitled A National
Profile of Black Youth: The Class of 1971. It's a nationwide, statistical survey of 54,720 black young people who
graduated from high school in 1971. Statistics on the
respondents' families, types of academic programs pursued,
overall ranks and grade point averages, years completed
and grade point averages in various subjects, future plans,
and opinions of society, are some of the topics surveyed.
   These statistics are presented in the following five
separate categories: by sex of student, family income,
head of household, region of residence, and number of
dependents in the family. Future research reports are
planned for this series to analyze various relationships
among the data presented in this first report.

(0125)

Ohio University, Athens. Center for Afro-
    American Studies. Afro-American Studies
    and Contemporary Issues. Athens, Ohio,
    Ohio University, Center for Afro-
    American Studies, [1972]. 3 vols.

    This manual for college and university Black Studies
courses can also be used as an effective reference tool.
Part I is a guide to discussions of several contemporary
issues in Black Studies such as the black family and black
identity. Part II entitled "People Pieces," provides
biographical profiles of 99 black Americans over the period
of 1770 to 1971. Material written by and/or about the subject of the profile is cited with each one. Part III includes discussions of several historical topics, such as the
New York African Free School and black music, which are of
interest to Black Studies. These two topics are among many
which are graphically displayed on a fold-out historical time
line chart which outlines Afro-American history from 1770
to 1971. Two other time line charts are included which outline the history of Afro-American authors and Afro-American
music respectively over the period of 1770 to 1971.

        (Same title cited at no. 022.)

(0126)

Southern Education Reporting Service.
    A Statistical Summary, State By State, Of
    School Segregation-Desegregation In The
    Southern and Border Area From 1954 - the
    Present. Nashville, Southern Education
    Reporting Service, 1967. 44 pp., tables.

    Includes regional and state-by-state statistical infor-
mation on the desegregation of students and faculty in
Southern school systems with generalized statistics on public colleges, and universities as of the 1966-67 academic
year.

(0127)

Tuskegee Institute, Dept. of Records and Research.
    A Selected List of References Relating to the
    Elementary, Secondary, and Higher Education of
    Negroes, 1949 to June 1955. Records and research
    pamphlet, No. 5. Tuskegee Institute, Ala., July,
    1955. 18ℓ.

    Most of the citations included in this eighteen page
bibliography are for periodical articles.

(0128)

Tuskegee Institute. Dept. of Records and
    Research. A Selected List of References
    Relating to the Negro Teacher, 1949 to
    June 1955. Records and research pamphlet
    No. 7, Tuskegee Institute, Ala., July,
    1955, 31.

    A very brief (three page) bibliography of primarily
periodical references on black educators.

(0129)

Weinberg, Meyer. The Education of the
    Minority Child; A Comprehensive
    Bibliography of 10,000 Selected
    Entries. Chicago, Integrated
    Education Associates, 1970.
    xii, 530 pp.

    Mexican, Indian, and other North American ethnic minori-
ties are represented in this bibliography of 10,000 references which emphasizes black Americans in its exploration of
specific and related issues in the education of minority
children.
    One of the major sections, "The American Scene," empha-
sizes current education issues and situations in forty-two
states plus the District of Columbia, with sub-sections on
Chicago and New York City. Another important section deals
with Afro-American studies and explores such issues as
culturally fair textbooks and the organization of black
studies programs. The final section lists 250 useful bibliographies for further research.

History

(0130)

Bergman, Peter M. The Chronological History
    of the Negro in America. New York, Harper &
    Row, [1969]. 698 pp.

    Covering the historical period from 1492 to 1968, this
chronological history of the black experience in the New
World is uneven in its treatment of the topics covered. At
times it is too sketchy. This wide-ranging survey notes such
events as the importation of slaves into Latin America in
1502 and the formation of the American Anti-Slavery Society
in 1833. Included in the more substantial sketches is a
description of the life and career of Adam Clayton Powell,
Sr. (1865-1953). The chronology continues through the 20th
century and ranges from the first sit-in demonstration staged
in a Chicago Loop restaurant (1943) to the assassination of
Martin Luther King, Jr., in 1968.

(0131)

Blacks in America; Bibliographical Essays, by
    James M. McPherson, et. al. Garden City,
    New York, Doubleday, 1971. xxii, 430 pp.

    Over 4,000 monographs and periodical citations, includ-
ing both primary and secondary sources, are included in a
chronological arrangement of bibliographic essays which ex-
plore the black American experience from its African background (1500) to black life styles of 1970. These topics
are reflected in various aspects of the dominant white
society vis-a-vis the status of blacks and the black response
to the situation (e.g. slavery and slave revolts) plus the
social, cultural and religious life developed by blacks within a segregated society (e.g. the black church and the Harlem Renaissance). This narrative bibliography attempts to
include every important work relevant to its scope published
through 1970 and can be used as a guide to research or course
design.

(0132)

Brown, Carol J. Afro-American History. Indiana
    University. Focus: Black America Bibliog-
    raphy Libraries and Focus: Black America,
    Summer, 1969. 43 pp.

    A general subject bibliography on black history, based
on the holdings of the Indiana University Libraries.

(0133)

Diggs, Irene. Chronology of Notable Events and
    Dates in the History of the African and His
    Descendants During the Period of Slavery and
    the Slave Trade. Washington, Association
    for the Study of Negro Life and History,
    1970. ii, 71 pp.

    A world-wide chronological outline covering the period
of 3500 B.C. to 1888 A.D. when slavery was abolished in
Brazil.

(0134)

Ducas, George and Charles Van Doren, eds.
    Great Documents in Black American History.
    Introd. by C. Eric Lincoln. New York,
    Praeger, [1970]. xv, 321 pp. illus., ports.

    Black American history speaks through this collection
of essays, letters, narratives, speeches, and other docu-
ments spanning the period of the 18th to the late 20th cen-
tury. Among others, Benjamin Banneker speaks in a letter to
Thomas Jefferson, Richard Wright describes How "Bigger" Was
Born, and Malcolm X speaks to the Harvard Law School Forum.
Some other voices of this historical experience include:
Oladah Equiano (Gustavas Vassa), James Forten, Martin
Robison Delany, W.E.B. Du Bois, Marcus Garvey, E. Franklin
Frazier, and Le Roi Jones.

    Although the index for this volume is limited in cover-
age, each document is preceded by an introduction placing it
in historical perspective.

(0135)

Eppse, Merl Raymond. A Guide to the Study of
    the Negro in American History. Revised and
    enlarged. Nashville, National Publication
    Co., [1953]. 186 pp.

    This topically organized manual, which includes bibliog-
raphic references for each topic covered, is a guide to research for students of black American history.

(0136)

Foner, Philip S. The Voice of Black America;
    Major Speeches by Negroes in the United
    States, 1797-1971. New York, Simon and
    Schuster. 1972 xv, 1215 pp.

    From the antebellum period (1797-1860) to the civil rights
and black power movements (1963-1971), this collection of
speeches by black Americans chronicles their struggle for
liberation from many forms of injustice.
    Most of the speeches are printed in an extracted form
but some appear in their entirety. In addition, each one is
preceded by a brief introduction giving biographical information on the speaker and placing the speech in historical
perspective

(0137)

Freidel, Frank B. The Negro and Puerto Rican in
     American History. Boston, Heath, [1964]. 27 pp.

     A very brief historical survey of these two minority
groups viewed as voluntary and involuntary immigrants to
this country.

(0138)

Jackson, Miles M., comp. and ed. A Bibliography
     of Negro History and Culture for Young
     Readers. Pittsburgh, Published for Atlanta
     University by the University of Pittsburgh
     Press, [1968]. xxxi, 134 pp.

     An annotated list of monographs, organized by broad
subject headings, identifying recommended elementary and
secondary school levels for the titles cited, in addition to
a list of audio-visual materials.

(0139)

National Council of the Churches of Christ in
     the United States of America. Department
     of Educational Development. Black Heritage
     Resource Guide: A Bibliography of the Negro
     in Contemporary America. New York, Council
     Press, 1970. 30 pp.

     Including a short section on the church and racism, this
is primarily an introductory teacher's guide for print and
non-print materials on black history.

(0140)

Negro History, 1553-1903; An Exhibition of Books,
     Prints, and Manuscripts From the Shelves of
     the Library Company of Philadelphia and the
     Historical Society of Pennsylvania...April
     17 to July 17, 1969. Philadelphia, Library
     Company of Philadelphia , 1969. v, 83 pp.

     A selective and descriptive listing of 16th to 19th
century publications, dealing with black history, that are
available in these two important collections.
          (Same title cited at no. 011.)

(0141)

Romero, Patricia W. I Too Am America: Documents
    From 1619 to the Present. International Library
    of Negro Life and History. New York, Publishers
    Co., [1868]. xv, 304 pp. illus., facsims., map.

    A collection of 292 letters, speeches, essays, and other
material primarily related to the black American struggle
for freedom and equality and authored by both blacks and
whites. Most of the documents have been edited and are non-
public but some court cases, laws, and similar material are
included. Examples of material included are a letter from
Frederick Douglass to his former master in 1848, an 1880
speech by Richard T. Greener supporting the migration of
blacks from the South to the North, and the Nobel Peace
Prize acceptance speech of Martin Luther King, Jr. in 1964.
The complete list of documents found in the table of contents
and the detailed index aid in the use of this volume as a
reference tool.
                (Same title cited at no. 37j.)

(0142)

Salk, Erwin A., Comp. A Layman's Guide to
    Negro History. New, enlarged edition.
    New York, McGraw-Hill, [1967]. xviii,
    196 pp.

    A general survey or "fact book" of Afro-American history
covering such areas as important dates in black history and
early black inventors.
    Also included are topical bibliographies designed to in-
troduce the layman to the contributions of blacks to this
society.

(0143)

Sloan, Irving J. Blacks in America, 1492-1970;
    A Chronology and Fact Book. 3rd ed. Dobbs
    Ferry, New York, Oceana, 1971. x, 149 pp.

    A factual survey which highlights (by date) some of the
important facts, events, and personalities of the Afro-American experience from 1442 to 1971. Some of the useful supplementary items included are: a compilation of statistical
information on Afro-Americans; lists of major black publications and organizations; and an outline of Afro-American
history.

Spangler, Earl. Bibliography of Negro History:
    Selected and Annotated Entries, General and
    Minnesota. Minneapolis, Ross and Haines,
    1963. vii, 101 pp.

    The first section of this two-part annotated bibliog-
raphy provides a variety of selected references to material
on the overall Afro-American experience in the United States
in general, and in selected states and localities. The
second, larger section cites a variety of sources (books,
clippings, periodical articles, etc.) pertaining to blacks
in Minnesota. In addition, a descriptive list of black
newspapers published in Minnesota from 1885 to 1963 is included.

Literature and Folklore

(0145)

Baker, Houston A., comp. Black Literature in
America. New York, McGraw-Hill, [1971].
xvi, 443 pp.

An anthology which emphasizes the folkloristic base and
socio-historical concerns of Afro-American literature and
also includes brief biographical sketches of the authors
included.

(0146)

Bone, Robert A. The Negro Novel in America.
Rev. ed. New Haven, Conn., Yale University Press, 1965. 289 pp.

An indexed, critical narrative on the development of the
Afro-American novel plus the cultural and social factors which
affected its development. An extensive bibliography is also
included.

(0147)

Chapman, Abraham. The Negro in American Literature and a Bibliography of Literature By
and About Negro Americans. Wisconsin Council
of Teachers of English. Special Publication
no. 15. [Oshkosh, Wis., Wisconsin Council
of Teachers of English. 1966]. 135 pp.

Including only citations to monographs, this bibliography, which was published in 1966 as a "work-in-progress,"
lacks an index and some of the titles cited lack complete
bibliographic information.
An exclusive subject arrangement is used including,
among other categories: fiction, literary criticism, and
biography. No separate sections are devoted exclusively
to a bibliographic survey of individual black authors as in
Darwin Turner's Afro-American Writers (no. 0165). However,
supplementary sections dealing with such topics as black
history, civil rights and education are included.

(0148)

Dace, Leticia. Le Roi Jones (Imamu Amiri Baraka):
A Checklist of Works By and About Him. London,
Wether Press, 1971. 196 pp.

This compilation includes content and detailed publication information, along with a list of reviews, for each of
Le Roi Jones' books and pamphlets listed. Among the other
bibliographic sections included are those on his writings
published in periodicals and his political and racial views.
--- See also: Hudson, Theodore R., A Le Roi Jones (Amiri
Baraka) bibliography (no. 0154).

(0149)

Deodene, Frank. Black American Fiction Since
1952; a Preliminary Checklist. Chatham,
N.J., The Chatham Bookseller, 1970. 25 pp.

The title of this short bibliography is quite descriptive.
Included, among others, are the works of Gordon Parks,
Richard Wright and W.E.B. DuBois, published from 1952 to
1970.

(0150)

Deodene, Frank and William P. French. Black
American Poetry Since 1944: A Preliminary
Checklist. Chatham, N.J., The Chatham
Bookseller, 1971. 41 pp.

An author list of all separately published books and
pamphlets (except those with fewer than five pages) by
Afro-American poets from 1944 to early 1971. Anthologies
devoted largely to modern Afro-American poetry are also included.

(0151)

Dickinson, Donald C. A Bio-bibliography of
Langston Hughes, 1902-1967. 2nd ed. rev.
Hamden, Conn., Archon Books, 1972. xiii,
273 pp., port.

This expansion of the author's library science dissertation combines a biography and comprehensive bibliographic
survey of the published works of Langston Hughes through
1965.

(0152)

Green, Elizabeth A.L. The Negro in Contemporary
    American Literature; an Outline for Individual
    and Group Study. 1928. Reprint. College Park,
    Md., McGrath, 1968. 92 pp.

    Essentially a course outline, this is an early 20th
century guide to the study of various aspects of literature
and drama by and about Afro-Americans.

(0153)

Haywood, Charles. A Bibliography of North American
    Folklore and Folksong. 2nd rev. ed. 2 vols.
    New York, Dover, 1961.

    In addition to a section dealing with blacks in the
West Indies, Vol. 1 of this bibliography includes an extensive section on the folklore, folksongs, spirituals, etc.
of blacks in the United States.

(0154)

Hudson, Theodore R. A Le Roi Jones (Amiri
    Baraka) Bibliography. A Keyed Research
    Guide to Works by Le Roi Jones and To
    Writing About Him and His Works.
    [Washington, 1971].

    Key symbols are used to identify the genre or literary
style of works by Le Roi Jones and the primary concern of
writings about him, in this brief bibliographic guide.---
See also: Dace, Leticia, Le Roi Jones (Imamu Amiri Baraka):
A Checklist...(no. 0148).

(0155)

Jahn, Janheinz. A Bibliography of Neo-African
    Literature from Africa, America, and the
    Caribbean. New York, Praeger, 1965 . xxxv,
    359 pp. map.

    The compiler of this bibliography defines Neo-African
literature as that which is written (as opposed to spoken),
has experienced certain Western influences, and contains
elements of style stemming from Negro-African oral tradi-
tions.
    Organized by broad geographical areas, the bibliography's
first section is devoted to Africa whereas the second and
third sections are devoted to Neo-African literature in the
Caribbean and in North America respectively. Listed in
each section are literary works published as monographs,
plays which have been performed, and completed manuscripts.
Anthologies and individual works are listed alphabetically
by editor or author. In the case of individual works, the
author's country of birth is indicated next to his name.

(0156)

Johnson, James Weldon, ed. The Book of
    American Negro Poetry, Chosen and Ed.
    with an Essay on the Negro's Creative
    Genius . . . New York, Harcourt, Brace
    and Co., 1922. xlviii, 217 pp.

    Paul Laurence Dunbar, James Weldon Johnson, and Claude
McKay are some of the earlier Afro-American poets covered
in this collection of selected poems.

(0157)

Levi, Doris J. and Nerissa L. Milton, comps.
    Directory of Black Literary Magazines.
    Focus: Series No. 1, Washington, D.C.,
    The Negro Bibliographic and Research
    Center, 1970. 19 pp.

    Descriptive information, including address, publisher,
subscription rates, etc., is presented for 47 black magazines containing poetry, fiction, book reviews and articles
on black literature.
                (Same title cited at No. 0172.)

(0158)

Perry, Margaret. A Bio-Bibliography of
    Countee P. Cullen, 1903-1946.
    Westport, Conn., Greenwood, 1971.
    xix, 134 pp.

    Including a section of biographical information on this
major black poet of the "Harlem Renaissance" period, plus
another section explaining his poetry, this bibliography
lists his major works in addition to reviews, and general
articles about Cullen and his poetry.

(0159)

Porter, Dorothy B. North American Negro Poets,
    A Bibliographical Checklist of Their
    Writings, 1760-1944. Heartman's Historical
    Series No. 70. Hattiesburg, Miss., The
    Book Farm, 1945. 90 pp.

    An alphabetical list (by author) of books, pamphlets,
and a few broadsides of poetry written primarily by blacks
born in the United States. Also included are some works of
poetry written by West Indians. Included with the usual
bibliographic information provided for each title, is the
notation of the presence of the poet's portrait in some of
the works cited. Both individual works and anthologies
written and edited respectively by black authors are
herein cited and symbols are used to indicate the location
of these titles in selected library collections throughout
the country. This checklist is an expansion and revision
of the 1916 publication: A Bibliographical Checklist of
American Negro Poetry, by Arthur A. Schomburg.

(0160)

Ryan, Pat M. Black Writing in the U.S.A.:
    A Bibliographic Guide. Brockport, N.Y.,
    Drake Memorial Library, 1969. v. ,
    48 pp.

    Four separate categories of material are cited in this
bibliographic guide. The initial section lists, alphabetically by institution, major United States archival collections on Afro-American history and literature. General
reference titles and bibliographies (from both periodicals
and monographs) are listed in the second section. A list
of black American periodicals, both current and out-of-
print, follows in the next section. The fourth section
cites literary, historical, and general anthologies which
deal with various aspects of the black American experience.

(0161)

Scally, Mary Anthony, Sister. Negro Catholic
    Writers, 1900-1943, A Bio-bibliography.
    Detroit, W. Romig & Co., [1945]. 152 pp.

    Seventy-four Afro-American authors who were also Roman
Catholics, are covered in this biographical and literary
survey covering the period 1900-1943. Personal and literary biographical information is provided for each author,
followed by annotated citations of their published works.
A subject index to authors and their works is also included.

(0162)

Smith, Gloria L. A Slice of Black Americana:
    A Regional Survey of History, A Chronology
    of Publications from 1746-1940, a Survey
    of Literary Genres for Teachers or Stu-
    dents of History and Literature. Champaign,
    Ill., University of Illinois, 1969. 38 ℓ.

    Afro-American literature is emphasized in this descrip-
tive and bibliographic survey of the black American historical and literary experience.

(0163)

Spalding, Henry D., comp. and ed. Encyclopedia
    of Black Folklore and Humor. Middle
    Village, New York, Jonathan David, 1972.
    xviii, 589 pp., illus.

    A compilation of black American folksongs, folktales,
poems, rhymes, etc., placed in the historical and cultural
perspective of the black experience in America.

(0164)

Swisher, Robert D. and Archer, Jill A., comps.
    Black American Literature, compiled by
    Robert Swisher/Black American Folklore,
    compiled by Jill A. Archer. Indiana
    University. Focus: Black America Bibli-
    ography Series. [Bloomington], Indiana
    University Libraries and Focus: Black
    America, Summer, 1969. 25 pp.

    Books published during the period of 1949-1969, by
black American authors and about their literature, make up
the first bibliography in this compilation based on material in the Indiana University Libraries. The second bibliography, on black folklore, also emphasizes material published in the post-1949 period but includes some important
works published prior to 1949 in its listing of both monographic and periodical literature.

(0165)

Turner, Darwin T.   Afro-American Writers.
    New York, Appleton-Century-Crofts,
    Educational Division, 1970.
    xvii, 117 pp.

    Both periodical and monographic literature is cited in
this bibliographic survey of Afro-American literature and
of individual black writers. Sections providing general
literary criticism plus historical, social, and cultural   °
background material are also included.
    Book length works are listed for each author included,
plus other bibliographies of their works, critical and
bibliographical references. (See also Chapman, Abraham,
The Negro in American Literature, No. 0147.)

(0166)

Whiteman, Maxwell.   A Century of Fiction by
    American Negroes, 1853-1952; A Descriptive
    Bibliography. Philadelphia, 1955.

    Including a chronology of Afro-American literature,
from the publication of Clotel by William Wells Brown in
1853 to the publication of several works in 1952, this is
a comprehensive, descriptive bibliography of fiction
written by black Americans. Periodical literature is
excluded unless an entire novel is included in a periodical.

Media (Press, Radio, and Television)

Black List; the Concise Reference Guide to
    Publications and Broadcasting Media of
    Black America, Africa and the Caribbean.
    N.Y., Panther House, [1971]. 289 pp.

    Including newspapers, broadcasting stations, univer-
sities, bookstores, and publishers, among others, this
guide provides such basic information as titles and addresses for publications of black Africa, the Caribbean,
and the United States.
    The international section includes a list of embassies
and permanent missions of independent Africa and the Caribbean to the United Nations.

Brown, Warren H. Checklist of Negro News-
    papers in the United States (1827-1946).
    Lincoln University Journalism Series,
    Jefferson City, Mo., School of Journalism,
    Lincoln University, 1946. 37 pp.

    This alphabetical list of 467 black American newspapers,
published from 1827 to 1946, includes the dates they were
founded and expired, editors' names, and the location of all
known copies.

Directory of National Black Periodicals and
    Journals. Issue no. 1-   , June 26, 1970-
        , New York, Afram Associates, 1970-
    Annual.

    An annual alphabetical list of Afro-American and black
African periodicals which includes subscription rates,
addresses, and the number of issues per year.

Hill, Roy L. Who's Who in the American Negro
    Press. Dallas, Royal Publishing, 1960.
    80 pp.

    Includes biographical information on editors, publish-
ers, writers, etc., connected with the black press as of
1960 in addition to a general critical survey of the black
press as of 1960.

(0171)

La Brie, Henry G. *The Black Newspaper in America; a Guide.* (Cover title: *The Black Press in America*). [Iowa City], Institute for Communication Studies, University of Iowa, 1970. 64 pp.

A state-by-state guide to current Afro-American newspapers which provides such basic information as title, address, publisher, and circulation.

(0172)

Levi, Doris J. and Nerissa L. Milton, comps. *Directory of Black Literary Magazines.* Focus: Series No. 1. Washington, D.C., The Negro Bibliographic and Research Center, 1970. 19 pp.

Descriptive information, including address, publisher, subscription rate, etc., is presented for 47 black magazines containing poetry, fiction, book reviews, and articles on black literature.
(Same title cited at no. 0157.)

(0173)

Pride, Armistead S., comp. *Negro Newspapers on Microfilm; a Selected List.* Washington, Library of Congress, Photoduplication Service, 1953.

Organized by city within each state, this is a selected list of black newspapers which were available on microfilm from the Library of Congress in 1953. The newspapers in this list are available on microfilm in the Newspaper Microtext Department of the Northwestern University Library.

(0174)

U.S. Bureau of the Census. *Negro Newspapers and Periodicals in the United States 1935-1940.* Washington, U.S. Bureau of the Census, 1935-1941.

The 1935 and 1936 editions of this now historical list provide the title, address, frequency of publication, and editor for black newspapers and magazines published in the U.S., plus a list of black press services. The editions published from 1937 to 1941 lack the names of the editors for the items listed but have the added feature of combined circulation statistics for black newspapers and periodicals plus statistical data on black press services.

(0175)

Wolseley, Roland E. The Black Press, U.S.A.
    Ames, Iowa State University Press, [1971].
    xiii, 362 pp. illus., ports.

    A short discussion of black radio is included in this
narrative survey of the history and current state of the
black press in the United States. Also included are short
histories of black magazines and newspapers.

(0176)

Yale University. Library. A Selected List of
    Periodicals Relating to Negroes, With
    Holdings in the Libraries of Yale Univer-
    sity. New Haven, Conn., Yale University
    Library, 1970. iv, 26 pp.

    Newspapers are excluded from this list which includes
historical publication information such as dates of publication and suspension for most of the titles listed.

Race Relations

(0177)

Connecticut. Inter-Racial Commission.
    Selected Bibliography for Inter-Racial
    Understanding. Hartford, Conn., Connect-
    icut Inter-Racial Commission, [1944]. 36 pp.

A short reading list for children and adults geared
to the promotion of racial harmony and understanding between blacks and whites.

(0178)

Detroit. Public Library. Race Restrictive
    Covenants; a Selected List of References.
    Detroit. Distributed by National Associa-
    tion for the Advancement of Colored People,
    [1946]. 8ℓ.

A useful list for historical purposes including books,
pamphlets, periodicals, and selected court cases.

(0179)

Flax, Michael J. Blacks and Whites; an
    Experiment in Racial Indicators.
    [Washington, Urban Institute, 1971]. 79 pp.

Income, housing, and education are some of the areas
explored in this statistical report which indicates certain measurable inequalities between blacks and whites
in 1960 and 1968.

(0180)

Grayshon, Matthew C. and V.P. Houghton.
    Initial Bibliography of Immigration and
    Race. Institute of Education. Educa-
    tional Papers, no. 6. Nottingham, Eng-
    land, University. Institute of Education
    1966, 38 pp.

Although compiled in response to immigration and related race-relations issues in Great Britain, a large percentage of the material cited was published in the U.S. and
deals with those issues in this country. Also of interest
are the studies dealing with West Indians and their migration to Great Britain.
    Education, psychology, and sociology are the basic sub-
ject categories used to cite, books, journal articles, theses, and other material. A separate listing is provided
for British government and United Nations Publications in
addition to another list of selected dissertations cited
in Dissertation Abstracts.

(0181)

Horowitz, Harold W. Law, Lawyers, and Social
    Change; Cases and Materials on the Abolition
    of Slavery, Racial Segregation, and Inequal-
    ity of Educational Opportunity. Indianapolis,
    Bobbs-Merrill, [1969]. xxiii, 531 pp.

    A law school text which explores various parts of the
legal system such as the courts, legislatures, and lawyers
as they apply to the social issues mentioned in the title.
Implementation, in the South, of the Supreme Court's 1954
decision of Brown v. Board of Education is one of the major
topics explored.

(0182)

Jackson, Giovanna R., comp. Afro-American
    Religion and Church and Race Relations.
    Indiana University. Focus: Black America
    Bibliography. Series. [Bloomington],
    Indiana, University Libraries and Focus:
    Black America, 1969. 18 pp.

    A brief bibliography of monographic material in the
Indiana University Libraries (as of Jan., 1969) dealing
with Afro-American religion and the experiences of non-
black denominations with racial issues.

(0183)

Thompson, Edgar T. and Alma M. Thompson, comps.
    Race and Region, a Descriptive Bibliography
    Compiled with Special Reference to the Re-
    lations Between Whites and Negroes in the
    United States. Chapel Hill, University of
    North Carolina Press, 1949. xii, 194 pp.

    A general bibliography on the black experience, covering
many subject categories such as: race relations, the black
experience in cities, racial conflict, and the language and
dialect of black Americans.

(0184)

Waxman, Julia. Race Relations; A Selected
    List of Readings on Racial and Cultural
    Minorities in the United States with
    Special Emphasis on Negroes. Chicago,
    Julius Rosenwald Fund, 1945. 47 pp.

    A brief historical and cultural bibliographic survey on
minorities in the United States with a specific section on
blacks and black-white relations.

Slavery

(0185)

Dumond, Dwight L. A Bibliography of Antislavery
    in America. Ann Arbor, University of
    Michigan Press, [1961]. 119 pp.

    An alphabetical list by author, title, or issuing agency
of all important American and British letters, debates,
tracts, etc. which were widely circulated in the United
States by activists in the antislavery movement.

(0186)

Oberlin College. Library. Microcard Collection
    of Anti-Slavery Propaganda in the Oberlin
    College Library, November, 1968. Louisville,
    Lost Cause Press, [1968]. 101 pp.

    Some pro-slavery and British anti-slavery propaganda is
included in this list of approximately 2,500 primarily anti-
slavery pamphlets, published in the United States before
1863. This collection, composed of annual reports, slave
narratives, and a variety of other material, is available on
microcard from Lost Cause Press.

(0187)

Thompson, Lawrence S. The Southern Black: Slave
    and Free; a Bibliography of Anti- and Pro-
    Slavery Books and Pamphlets, and of Social
    and Economic Conditions in the Southern
    States from the Beginnings to 1950. Troy,
    N.Y., Whitston, 1970. 576 pp.

    Compiled from a number of sources including: E.M.
Coulter's Travels in the Confederate States and a large portion of the Oberlin College Library's slavery collection.

(0188)

Tragle, Henry I., comp. The Southampton Slave
    Revolt of 1831; a Compilation of Source
    Material. Amherst, University of Massachu-
    setts Press, 1971. xviii, 489 pp., facsims,
    map.

    Newspaper accounts, verbatim trial records, and other
selected published accounts, are some of the items included
in this major work on the slave revolt led by Nat Turner in
Southampton County, Virginia.

Society and Culture

(0189)

Baskin, Wade. Dictionary of Black Culture.
     New York, Philosophical Library, [1953].
     493 pp.

     Entries for individuals are emphasized in this historical
and contemporary dictionary which also includes events, organizations, institutions, and publications of and/or about
black America. Many of the entries, particularly those for
individuals, lack the adequate identification of dates and
related information, which would provide more definite historical identification.
     (Same title cited at numbers 016 and 031.)

(0190)

The Black Family and the Black Woman, a
     Bibliography. [Bloomington, Ind.,
     Indiana University], 1972.

     The first section of this bibliography, based on the
holdings of the Indiana University Library, deals with the
black family and begins with a sub-section of historical
background information. Monographs, periodical articles,
and government publications are then cited in a survey of
the black American family in the twentieth century.
     Section two also cites general background and historical
material in its bibliographic survey of American black women.
Monographs and periodical articles are cited in a topical
arrangement covering such areas as identity and liberation,
autobiography and biography, and literature by black women.

(0191)

Boyce, Byrl N. Minority Groups and Housing; a
     Bibliography, 1950-1970.[Morristown, N.J.],
     [1972]. 202 pp.

     Including an excellent subject index and an author index,
this is an updated and expanded version of an earlier bibliography (Messner, Stephen D. Minority Groups and Housing ...
no. 0200). Housing discrimination, and other issues dealing
with minority groups and housing, are explored through this
annotated bibliography of books, periodical articles, pamphlets, reports, and films. There are also two sections
that deal specifically with legislation and legal action
affecting minority groups and housing.

(0192)

California. Department of Industrial Relations.
     Division of Labor Statistics and Research.
     Negroes and Mexican Americans in South and
     East Los Angeles; Changes Between 1960 and
     1965 in Population, Employment, Income,
     and Family Status. An Analysis of a U.S.
     Census Survey of November, 1965. San
     Francisco, State of California, Division of
     Fair Employment Practices, 1966. 40 pp., map.

     This statistical survey indicates that while the nation
and California prospered economically from 1960 to 1965, the
economic conditions of a large portion of the black and
Spanish surnamed population of Los Angeles worsened or, at
best, did not improve.

(0193)

Cameron, Colin. Minorities in the Armed Forces; a
     Selected, Occasionally Annotated Bibliography.
     Madison, Wisconsin, University of Wisconsin,
     Institute for Research on Poverty, 1970. 32ℓ.

     A bibliographic outline of the situations faced by
minority group servicemen before, during, and after their
military tours of duty.

(0194)

Jackson, Giovanna R. and Sweet, Charles E., comps.
     Black Nationalism, compiled by Giovanna R.
     Jackson/The Negro and the Establishment: Law
     Politics and the Courts, compiled by Charles E.
     Sweet. Indiana University. Focus: Black America
     Bibliography Series. [Bloomington], Indiana
     University Libraries and Focus: Black America,
     Summer, 1969. 28 pp.

     Primarily recently published (1958-68) monographs and
periodical articles on topics such as black consciousness,
the black Muslim movement, and the back to Africa movements
are explored under the broad concept of black nationalism in
the first bibliography of this compilation. The second,
brief bibliography concentrates on monographs in its exploration of the black experience with the law, legislators, and
the courts in areas ranging from slavery, to civil liberties,
and to the police.

(0195)

Johnson, Jesse J. The Black Soldier (Documented
   1619-1815); Missing Pages in United States
   History. Hampton, Va., Hampton Institute,
   [1969]. xii, 174 pp.
Through this selective compilation of complete and ex-
cerpted documents, dealing with the black soldier from 1619
to 1815, the author pursues his thesis that historically the
U.S. military has rejected blacks during peace, recruited
them during wartime, and again rejected them after war.

(0196)

Johnson, Jesse J. The Black Soldier (Documented,
   1619-1815); Missing Pages in United States
   History. Rev. Ed. Hampton, Va. Hampton Institute,
   [1970]. 79 pp. illus.

The revised edition of this title provides a different
arrangement of material plus introductory comments before
each document, as opposed to the consolidated section of
comments in the 1969 edition.

(0197)

Johnston, Percy E., ed. Afro-American Philosophies;
   Selected Readings, from Jupiter Hammon to
   Eugene C. Holmes. Upper Montclair, N.J.,
   Montclair State College Press, 1969. ix, 77 pp.

Through the use of an anthology of selected writing and
addresses of the blacks included, the editor attempts to
provide insight into black American philosophical thought.
   The work is prefaced by a list of short biographical
sketches of the individuals included.

(0198)

Joint Center for Political Studies. [Guide to Black
   Politics '72.] The Joint Center for Political
   Studies Guide to Black Politics '72. Washington, The Joint Center for Political Studies, 1972.
   2 vols. illus.

   Designed as an informational guide for black delegates
to the Democratic and Republican National Conventions of 1972.
While volumes one and two deal respectively with the Democratic and Republican Conventions, they both provide the same
type of information for these conventions plus non-partisan
information on black politics. Some of the items covered are
general convention procedures, a state-by-state list of black
delegates and alternates to both conventions plus the names
of blacks on standing committees.
   Such non-partisan information as statistics on the black
voting age population in major cities and in all states, is
supplied in a section on the potential influence of the black
vote in 1972. Included in statistical tables on U.S. Con-
gressional districts with black populations of 30 per cent
or more, are such statistics as the total black voting age
population by district. Among the items included in the
appendix is a list of black members of the U.S. Congress
from 1869 to 1973 with their terms of office.

(0199)

Major, Clarence. Dictionary of Afro-American
   Slang. New York, International Publishers,
   1970. 127 pp. (British ed. published in
   1971 under the title: Black Slang: A Dictionary of Afro-American Talk. London,
   Routledge and K. Paul, 1971. 127 pp.)

   Nicknames are included in this dictionary of slang words
and phrases which have originated both within and outside of
black communities, but have enjoyed popular usage among black
Americans. Where it could be determined, dates of popular
usage for the words and phrases defined are included.

(0200)

Messner, Stephen D. Minority Groups and
     Housing; a Selected Bibliography, 1950-67.
     University of Connecticut. Center for Real
     Estate and Urban Economic Studies. General
     Series, no. 1 [Storrs, Conn., University
     of Connecticut, Center for Real Estate and
     Urban Economic Studies, 1968]. vii, 60 pp.

     Through a variety of published and unpublished material,
this topical bibliography explores assorted causes and effects
of housing integration and segregation, viewed from a perspective of open-access housing for all. For more expanded coverage see the later edition of this title: Boyce, Byrl N.,
Minority Groups and Housing; a Bibliography ... no. 0191.

(0201)

Miller, Kent S. and Ralph M. Dreger, eds.
     Comparative Studies of Blacks and Whites
     in the United States. [Seminar Press.
     Quantitative Studies in Social Relations.]
     New York, Seminar Press, 1973. xiii, 572 pp.

     Sixteen major topics are explored, in separate chapters,
in this critical survey of recent (1966-1971) comparative
psychological, sociological, and physiological research on
black and white Americans. The research surveyed has been
based on the realization of the existence of two separate
cultures in the United States. Some of the topics explored
include: language abilities of black Americans, intellectual
functioning, extent and effects of desegregation, occupational
aspirations, family organization, and black crime.
     In discussing, summarizing, and indicating future trends
of research in each of these areas, the contributors discuss
specific studies cited in a bibliography at the end of each
chapter.

(0202)

Morris, Milton D. The Politics of Black America:
     an Annotated Bibliography. Carbondale, Public
     Affairs Research Bureau, Southern Illinois
     University at Carbondale, 1971. xiii, 84 pp.

     Black political participation and leadership are two of
the topics covered in this bibliographic exploration of the
effects of race relations on the political processes and
institutions of the U.S. plus the use of politics by black
Americans to change unacceptable conditions.

(0203)

Roberts, Hermese E. The Third Ear: A Black
    Glossary. [Chicago, The English Language
    Institute of America, 1971. 15 pp.]

    A guide to the meaning of selected words and phrases of
slang as they have developed and been used in black American
communities. The terms are briefly defined and usually
identified as to their usage as parts of speech. Cross references from one term to another are extensively used throughout
as well as the listing of synonyms for many terms.

(0204)

Southern Regional Council. Voter Education Pro-
    ject (1966-   ). Black Elected Officials
    in the Southern States. Atlanta Southern
    Regional Council. Voter Education Project,
    [1969]. iii, 24 pp.

    Black southerners, who held elected public office as of
late 1968 are listed along with their addresses plus the name
of the office held.

(0205)

Sprecher, Daniel. Guide to Films (16 mm) About
    Negroes. Alexandria, Va., Serina Press,
    [1970]. vi, 87 pp.

    Most of the films in this annotated, alphabetical list
are black and white with sound. Running time, date of re-
lease, and recommended school grade levels are indicated for
most films listed. Africa, the Black Panthers, civil rights,
racial discrimination, and urban life are just a few of the
topics covered as indicated by the subject index. Each film
is keyed to a list of commercial sources as an aid to their
acquisition.

(0206)

Sweet, Charles E., comp. Sociology of the
    American Negro. Indiana University.
    Focus: Black America Bibliography Series.
    [Bloomington], Indiana University Libraries
    and Focus: Black America, Summer, 1969.
    53 pp.

    Race problems, segregation, civil rights, and black
history are some of the topics explored in this selective
bibliography (emphasizing material published from 1948 to
1968, available in the Indiana University Libraries) which
the introduction describes as being related to the view
sociologists hold of American blacks.

(0207)

Swisher, Robert D. and Sweet Charles[E.],
       comps. Psychology of the Black American,
       compiled by Robert Swisher/Biological As-
       pects of Race, compiled by Charles [E.] Sweet.
       Indiana University. Focus: Black America
       Bibliography Series. [Bloomington], Indiana
       University Libraries and Focus: Black America,
       Summer, 1969. 26 pp.

       Both bibliographies in this compilation include recent
material based on the holdings of the Indiana University
Libraries. The first title covers such topics as ethnic
attitudes, intelligence levels, and child study under the
broad concept of the psychology of black Americans. The
second compilation, Biological Aspects of Race, is organized
by form of the material cited (i.e. monographs and journal
articles) with a separate list of journals cited.

(0208)

Tumin, Melvin M. Segregation and Desegregation,
       a Digest of Recent Research. [New York, Anti-
       Defamation League of B'nai B'rith, 1957.]
       112 pp.

       Professional journals form the primary basis for this
compilation of digests of research or research-related studies
from 1951 to 1956, covering such topics as the factors which
affect the process of desegregation.

(0209)

U.S. Bureau of the Census. Negro Population 1790-
       1915. Prep. by Dr. John Cummings. 1918.
       Reprint, New York, Kraus Reprint, 1969. 844 pp.
       illus., diagrs., maps., tables.

       Distribution and composition of the black population;
occupations; birth and mortality; and education, are some
of the areas surveyed in this special statistical survey of
black America from 1790 to 1915, issued by the U.S. Census
Bureau in 1918.
       Regular decennial censuses; other previously published
and unpublished census data; plus special original compila-
tions, were used as sources of information in this survey of
125 years of the black American experience.

(0210)

U.S. Bureau of the Census. <u>Negroes in the</u>
<u>United States, 1920-1932</u>. Prep. by Charles
E. Hall. Washington, Govt. Print. Off., 1935.
xvi, 845 pp. maps, tables, diagrs.

Similar in scope to the Census Bureau's earlier compilation, <u>Negro Population 1790-1915</u> (no. 0209), this statistical
survey of black America covers the period of 1920 to 1932.
Also based on some previously published and unpublished
census data, this compilation explores the similar areas of
vital statistics; population growth by decade; business and
agriculture; etc., that were covered in the 1915 survey. Most
of the latest statistics in this volume are from 1930. A
useful appendix is a survey of selected characteristics of the
black population by counties in 1930. This is a more extensive survey than a similar section of statistical tables in
the 1918 compilation.

(0211)

Williams, Ethel L. <u>Afro-American Religious Studies</u>:
<u>a Comprehensive Bibliography with Locations</u>
<u>in American Libraries</u>. Metuchen, N.J.,
Scarecrow Press, 1972. 454 pp.

Five general topical categories, including one on the
Afro-American religious experience, are further sub-divided in
this comprehensive bibliographic survey of African and Afro-
American religious studies which also provides at least·one
library location for each item cited.

(0212)

Williams, Ora. <u>American Black Women In the Arts</u>
<u>and Social Sciences: A Bibliographic Sur-</u>
<u>vey</u>. Metuchen, N.J., Scarecrow, 1973. xix,
141 pp. ports.

A period exceeding the last 200 years of the black American experience is spanned in this bibliography of over 1000
entries listing printed and audiovisual works written by and/
or about black American women. A topical arrangement is used
to cite reference works, biographical studies, anthologies,
dramatic and literary works, and other cultural studies.
Social and historical studies are also included in addition to
a few selected portraits of black women.

ADDENDUM

(A list of titles recently announced for publication)

(0213)

Afro-Americana, 1553-1906: Author Catalog of the
     Library Company of Philadelphia and the
     Historical Society of Pennsylvania. Boston,
     G.K.Hall, In Press. 728 pp.

(0214)

Aptheker, Herbert. Annotated Bibliography of the
     Published Writing of W.E.B. Du Bois. Millwood,
     New York, Kraus-Thompson, 1973.

(0215)

Dictionary Catalog of the Negro Collection of the
     Fisk University Library. Boston, G.K.Hall,
     6 vols.

(0216)

Encyclopedia of the Negro in Africa and America.
     St. Clair Shores, Michigan, Negro History
     Press, In Press, 18 vols.

(0217)

Schockley, Ann A. and Sue P. Chandler, eds.
     Living Black American Authors: A Biographi-
     cal Directory. Ann Arbor, R.R. Bowker, 1973.
     160 pp.

AUTHOR INDEX

Adams, A. 089

American Civil
Liberties Union.......090

Aptheker, Herbert.....0214

Archer, Jill A. 0164

Atlanta University......01

Baatz, Wilmer H. 0104

Baker, Augusta........051

Baker, Houston.......0145

Barker, Lucius J. 091

Barker, Twiley W.,
Jr. 091

Baskin, Wade.............
..........016, 031, 0189

Bell and Howell/
Atlanta University......01

Bell, Barbara L. 017

Bengelsdorf, Winnie...0112

Bergman, Peter M. 0130

Bone, Robert A. 0146

Boyce, Byrl N. 0191

Brooks, Alexander D. ..092

Brown, Carol J. 0132

Brown, Roscoe C. 042

Brown, Warren H. 0168

Calif. Dept. of
Industrial Relations,
Division of Labor
Statistics & Research.....0192

Calif. San Fernando
Valley State College,
Los Angeles. Library........052

Calif. State College,
Fresno. Library...........053

Calif. State College,
San Diego. Library........054

Cameron, Colin...........0193

Cederholm, Theresa D. 096

Chandler, Sue P. 0217

Chapman, Abraham.........0147

Chicago Public Library
Omnibus Project............048

Chilton, John.............097

Connecticut. Inter-
Racial Commission.........0177

Cummings, John............0209

Dace, Leticia.............0148

Davis, John P. 032

Davis, Russell H. 018

Davison, Ruth M. 055

Deodene, Frank.
Black American Poetry......0149

75

Deodene, Frank.
Black American
Fiction Since
1944.................0150

Detroit Public
Library..............0178

Dickinson, Donald C. .0151

Diggs, Irene.........0133

Dreger, Ralph M. 0201

Du Bois, W.E.B.
Encyclopedia of the
Negro................035

Du Bois, W.E.B., ed.
A Select Bibliography
of The Negro
American..............056

Ducas, George........0134

Dumond, Dwight L. ...0185

Ebony.................034

Edmonds, Helen G. 019

Egerton, John........0113

Ellis, Ethel M.V. 057

Eppse, Merl R. 0135

Feather, Leonard G.
The Encyclopedia
of Jazz...............098

Feather, Leonard G.
The Encyclopedia of
Jazz in the Sixties....099

Fichter, Joseph H.
Graduates of
Predominantly Negro
Colleges.............0114

Fichter, Joseph H.
Negro Women Bachelors.....0115

Fichter, Joseph H.
Young Negro Talent.......0116

Fisher, Mary L. 064

Fisk University.
Library.................0215

Flax, Michael J. 0179

Foner, Philip S. 0136

Foreman, Paul B. 058

Freidel, Frank B. 0137

French, William P. 0150

Friedman, Leon............093

Gold, Robert S. 0100

Grayshon, Matthew C. 0180

Green, Elizabeth A.L. 0152

Guzman, Jessie P. 095

Haley, James T. 036

Hall, Charles E. 0210

Hampton Institute,
Hampton, Va.
A Classified Catalogue
of the Negro Collection.....04

Hampton Institute,
Hampton, Va.
Dictionary Catalog of
the George Peabody
Collection.................05

Hatch, James V. 0101

Haywood, Charles.........0153

Heartman, Charles F. 06

Henderson, Edwin B. ..037g

Hicks, Richard........026

Hill, Mozell C. 058

Hill, Roy L. 0170

Historical Records
Survey. District
of Columbia............07

Historical Records
Survey. New York
(City)................08

Historical Society of
Pennsylvania. Negro
History, 1553-
1903..........011 & 0140

Historical Society of
Pennsylvania. Afro-
Americana, 1553-
1906................0213

Horowitz, Harold W. ..0181

Howard Univ.,
Wash., D.C. Library.....09

Houghton, V.P. 0180

Howard Univ.,
Wash., D.C. Library.
Moorland Foundation....010

Hudson, Theodore R. ..0154

Intensive Summer
Studies Program.......0118

International Library
of Negro Life and
History..............037

Irvine, Betty Jo......0102

Irwin, Leonard B. 059

Jackson, Giovanna R.
Afro-American
Religion.................0182

Jackson, Giovanna R.
Black Nationalism........0194

Jackson, Miles M. 0138

Jahn, Janheinz...........0155

Jay, James M. 0119

Johnson, Guy B. 035

Johnson, Harry A. 0120

Johnson, James Welson.....0156

Johnson, Jesse J.
The Black Soldier...
(1st ed.)................0195

Johnson, Jesse J.
The Black Soldier...
(Rev. ed.)...............0196

Johnston, Percy E. 0197

Joint Center for
Political Studies........0198

Kaiser, Ernest...........043

Kinton, Jack F. 060

Koblitz, Minnie W. 0121

Krash, Ronald............061

La Brie, Henry G. 0171

Lawson, Hilda J. 0103

Legler, April............055

Levi, Doris........0157 & 0172

Lewinson, Paul............062

Library Co. of
Philadelphia.
Negro History,
1553-1903.......011 & 0140

Library Co. of
Philadelphia.
Afro-Americana.......0213

Major, Clarence......0199

Marshall, A.P. 049

McCabe, Jane A.
Black Entertainers....0104

McCabe, Jane A.
Education and the
Afro-American........0122

McCabe, Jane A.
Music and the
Black American.......0102

McPherson, James M. ..0131

Merriam, Alan P. 0105

Messner, Stephen D. ..0200

Metcalf, George R. 020

Michalak, Thomas J. ..0106

Miller, Elizabeth W.
The Negro In
America...(1st ed.)....063

Miller, Elizabeth W.
The Negro in
America...............064

Miller, Kent S. 0201

Milton, Nerissa L. ....
..............0157 & 0172

Morais, Herbert M. ...037h

Morris, Milton D. 0202

National Alliance
of Businessmen...........0123

National Council of
the Churches of Christ
in the U.S.A. Dept.
of Educational
Development..............0139

National Minority
Business Direc-
tories, Inc. 0107

National Scholarship
Service for Negro
Students.................0124

National Urban League.
Dept. of Research.
Selected Bibliography
on the Negro. 3rd. ed. 065

National Urban League.
Dept. of Research.
Selected Bibliography
on the Negro. 4th ed. 066

National Urban League.
Dept. of Research.
Source Materials On
the Urban Negro...........067

Negro Bibliographic
and Research Center........069

New Jersey Library
Assoc. Bibliography
Committee.................070

New York (City).
City University of
New York..................071

New York (City)
Public Library. No
Crystal Stair; A
Bibliography..............072

New York. Public Library. Schomburg Collection of Negro Literature and History. Dictionary Catalog. Supplement I. ....012 & 013

Northrup, Henry D. 041

Oberlin College. Library...............0186

Ohio University, Athens.........022 & 0125

Patterson, Lindsay. An Introduction to Black Literature in America...............037f

Patterson, Lindsay. Anthology of the American Negro in the Theatre..037e

Patterson, Lindsay. Negro in Music and Art..................037d

Perry, Margaret.......0158

Ploski, Harry A. The Negro Almanac (1st ed.)..............042 (2nd ed.)..............043

Porter, Dorothy B. The Negro in the United States ; A Selected Biblio- graphy................073

Porter, Dorothy B. North American Negro Poets...........0159

Porter, Dorothy B. A Working Biblio- graphy on the Negro in the United States...074

Pride, Armistead S. ..0173

Prince George's County Memorial Library. Selective List of Government Publi- cations. (1969 ed.).......075

Prince George's County Memorial Library. Selective List of Government Publi- cations. (1970 ed.).......076

Race Relations Information Center........014

Rather, Ernest R. 044

Roberts, Hermese E. 0203

Robinson, Wilhelmena S. ...023 (for annotation), 37j

Rogers, Joel A. World's Great Men of Color..................024

Rogers, Joel A. 100 Amazing Facts About the Negro................045

Romero, Patricia W. I Too Am America.........0141 (for annotation), 37j

Romero, Patricia W. Negro Americans in the Civil War............037b

Ross, Franklin A. 078

Ryan, Pat M. 0160

Salk, Erwin A. 0142

Scally, Mary Anthony, Sister....................0161

Shockley, Ann A. 0217

Sloan, Irving J. 0143

Smith, Gloria L. 0162

Sobel, Lester A. 094

Southern Education
Reporting Service.....0126

Southern Regional
Council. Voter
Education Project
(1966-)..............0204

Spalding, Henry D. ...0163

Spangler, Earl.......0144

Spradling, Mary M. 025

Sprecher, Daniel......0205

Sturges, Gladys M. 077

Sweet, Charles E.
Biological Aspects
of Race...............0207

Sweet, Charles E.
The Negro and the
Establishment........0194

Sweet, Charles E.
Sociology of the
American Negro........0206

Swisher, Robert D.
Black American
Biography..............026

Swisher, Robert D.
Black American
Literature...........0164

Swisher, Robert D.
Psychology of the
Black American.......0207

Szabo, Andrew.........054

Tennessee Dept. of
Education. Division
of School Libraries....079

Texas Southern
University. Library.
Heartman Negro
Collection................015

Thompson, Alma M. 0183

Thompson, Edgar T. 0183

Thompson, Lawrence S. 0187

Toppin, Edgar A. 027

Tragle, Henry I. 0188

Treworgy, Mildred L. 080

Tullis, Carol............026

Tumin, Melvin M. 0208

Turner, Darwin T. 0165

Tuskegee Institute.
Dept. of Records and
Research. Civil Rights
and the Negro.............095

Tuskegee Institute.
Dept. of Records and
Research. A Selected
List of References
Relating to the
Elementary, Secondary,
and Higher Education
of Negroes...............0127

Tuskegee Institute.
Dept. of Records and
Research. A Selected
List of References
Relating to the
Negro Teacher...........0128

U.S. Air Forces
in Europe.................081

U.S. Bureau of
Apprenticeship and
Training.................0109

U.S. Bureau of
the Census. Negro
Newspapers and
Periodicals..........0174

U.S. Bureau of the
Census. Negro
Population 1790-1915..0209

U.S. Bureau of the
Census. Negroes in
the United States,
1920-1932............0210

U.S. Bureau of
Foreign and
Domestic Commerce.....0110

U.S. Library of
Congress. Division
of Bibliography........082

Van Doren, Charles....0134

Walters, Mary D. 083

Waxman, Julia.........0184

Weinberg, Meyer.......0129

Welsch, Erwin K. 084

Wesley, Charles H.
In Freedom's
Footsteps............037a

Wesley, Charles H.
Negro Americans in
the Civil War.........037b

Wesley, Charles H.
The Quest for
Equality.............037c

West, Earle H. A
Bibliography of
Doctoral Research
on the Negro..........085

West, Earle H. A
Bibliography of
Doctoral Research
on the Negro.
Supplement.................086

Whiteman, Maxwell........0166

Williams, Daniel T. 087

Williams, Ethel L.
Afro-American Religious
Studies..................0211

Williams, Ethel L.
Biographical Directory
of Negro Ministers.
(1st. ed.)................029

Williams, Ethel L.
Biographical Directory
of Negro Ministers.
(2nd. ed.)................030

Williams, Ora............0212

Wood, Robert S. 0104

Wolseley, Roland E. 0175

Work, Monroe N. 088

Wright, Richard R. 046

Yale University.
Library..................0176

TITLE INDEX

Afro-American Artists:
A Bio-Bibliographical
Directory...............096

Afro-American Biblio-
graphy; List of the
Books, Documents, and
Periodicals on Black
Culture Located in
San Diego State
College Library........054

Afro-American
Encyclopedia...........036

Afro-American History..0132

Afro-American Philo-
sophies; Selected
Readings...............0197

Afro-American
Religion and Church
and Race Relations.....0182

Afro-American Religious
Studies: A Comprehensive
Bibliography With Loca-
tions in American
Libraries..............0211

Afro-American Studies
and Contemporary
Issues..........022 & 0125

Afro-American Writers..0165

Afro-Americana, 1553-
1901; Author Catalog
of the Library Co.
of Philadelphia........0213

Afro-Americana: A
Comprehensive
Bibliography of
Resource Materials
in the Ohio State
Univ. Libraries...........083

Afro- and Mexican-
Americana: Books and
Other Materials...........053

American Black Women
in the Arts and Social
Sciences: A Biblio-
graphic Survey............0212

American Civil
Liberties Union
Papers: A Guide..........090

American Ethnic
Groups: A Sourcebook.......060

American Negro: A
Selected Checklist
of Books..................057

American Negro
Reference Book............032

Annotated Bibliography
of the Published
Writings of
W.E.B. Du Bois...........0214

Anthology of the
American Negro in
The Theatre..............037e

Bibliography of
Antislavery in
America..................0185

Bibliography of
Doctoral Research
on the Negro,
1933-1966.............085

Bibliography of
Doctoral Research
on the Negro,
Supplement, 1967-
1969..................086

Bibliography of Jazz..0105

Bibliography of Negro
History and Culture
for Young Readers.....0138

Bibliography of Negro
History: Selected and
Annotated Entries,
General and
Minnesota.............0144

Bibliography of Negro
Migration.............078

Bibliography of
Neo-African Literature
from Africa, America,
and the Caribbean.....0155

Bibliography of North
American Folklore and
Folksong..............0153

Bibliography of the
Negro in Africa and
America...............088

Bibliography of the
Black American........081

Bio-bibliography of
Countee P. Cullen,
1903-1946.............0158

Bio-bibliography of
Langston Highes,
1902-1967.............0151

Biographical
Directory of
Negro Ministers
(1st. ed.)............029

Biographical
Directory of
Negro Ministers
(2nd. ed.)............030

Biographical History
of Blacks in America
Since 1528............027

Biological Aspects
of Race...............0207

Black America: A
Research Bibliography......061

Black American Athletes...0104

Black American Biography...026

Black American Fiction
Since 1952; A Pre-
liminary Checklist.......0149

Black American Folklore...0164

Black American
Literature...............0164

Black American Poetry
Since 1944; A Prelim-
inary Checklist..........0150

Black American Scientists..026

Black Americans in
Public Affairs...........025

Black Athlete: Emergence
and Arrival..............037g

Black Biographical
Sources: An Annotated
Bibliography.............017

Black Culture Collection....01

Black Elected
Officials in the
Southern States.......0204

Black Entertainers
and the Entertain-
ment Industry........0104

Black Experience in
Children's Books.......051

Black Experience in
the United States; A
Bibliography Based on
Collections of the
San Fernando Valley
College Library.......052

Black Faces in High
Places; Negroes in
Government............019

Black Family and The
Black Woman, A
Bibliography.........0190

Black Heritage Resource
Guide: A Bibliography
of the Negro in
Contemporary America..0139

Black Image on the
American Stage: A
Bibliography of Plays
and Musicals, 1770-
1970.................0101

Black Information
Index..................047

Black List; the
Concise Reference
Guide to Publica-
tions and Broad-
casting Media of
Black America,
Africa and the
Caribbean............0167

Black Literature
in America...........0145

Black Nationalism.........0194

Black Newspaper in
America; A Guide.........0171

Black Perspectives:
A Bibliography............071

Black Press, U.S.A. 0175

Black Slang: A
Dictionary of Afro-
American Talk.............0199

Black Soldier
(Documented 1619-
1815). (1st. ed.)........0195

Black Soldier
(Documented 1619-
1915). (Rev. ed.)........0196

Black Studies:
A Bibliography............059

Black Writing in the
U.S.A.; A Biblio-
graphic Guide.............0160

Blacks and Whites;
an Experiment in
Racial Indicators.........0179

Blacks in America;
Bibliographical Essays....0131

Blacks in America, 1492-
1970; A Chronology and
Fact Book.................0143

Book of American
Negro Poetry..............0156

Calendar of the
Writing of Frederick
Douglass in the
Frederick Douglass
Memorial Home,
Anacosta, D.C. 07

Calendar of the
Manuscripts in the
Schomburg Collection....08

Catalogue: Heartman
Negro Collection.......015

Century of Fiction
by American Negroes,
1853-1952; A Des-
criptive Biblio-
graphy...............0166

Chance to Go to
College: A Directory
of 800 Colleges that
have Special Help for
Students from Minori-
ties and Low Income
Families.............0111

Checklist of Negro
Newspapers in the
United States (1827-
1946)................0168

Chicago Afro-American
Union Analytic
Catalog................02

Chicago Negro Almanac..044

Chronological
History of the
Negro in America......0130

Chronology of Notable
Events and Dates in
the History of the
African and His Des-
cendants During the
Period of Slavery and
the Slave Trade.......0133

Civil Liberties and
the Constitution.......091

Civil Rights and
Liberties in the
United States.........092

Civil Rights and the
Negro; A List of
References Relating
to Present Day
Discussions...............095

Civil Rights; A
Current Guide to the
People, Organizations,
and Events................089

Civil Rights, 1960-66......094

Civil Rights Reader;
Basic Documents of the
Civil Rights Movement......093

Classified Catalogue of
the Negro Collection
in the Collis P.
Huntington Library,
Hampton Institute...........04

College of Life: Or
Practical Self-Educator....041

Comparative Studies of
Blacks and Whites in
the United States........0201

Dictionary Catalog of
the Arthur B. Spingarn
Collection of Negro
Authors....................09

Dictionary Catalog of
the George Peabody
Collection of Negro
Literature and History......05

Dictionary Catalog of
the Jesse E. Moorland
Collection of Negro
Life and History,
Howard Univ.,
Washington, D.C. 010

Dictionary Catalog of
the Negro Collection
of the Fisk University
Library..................0215

Dictionary Catalog
of the Schomburg
Collection of
Negro Literature
and History...........012

Dictionary Catalog
of the Schomburg
Collection of
Negro Literature
and History.
Supplement I. 013

Dictionary of Afro-
American Slang.......0199

Dictionary of Black
Culture.....016, 031, 0189

Directory for
Reaching Minority
Groups...............0109

Directory: National
Black Organizations....033

Directory of Afro-
American Resources.....014

Directory of Afro-
Americana in Chicago
Area Libraries..........03

Directory of Black
Literary
Magazines......0157 & 0172

Directory of National
Black Periodicals &
Journals..............0169

Directory of Pre-
dominantly Black
Colleges and
Universities in the
United States of
America..............0123

Economic Status and
Conditions of the
Negro................0106

Education and the
Afro-American............0122

The Education of the
Minority Child; A
Comprehensive Biblio-
graphy of 10,000
Selected Entries.........0129

Eight Negro
Bibliographies.............087

Encyclopedia of
Black Folklore and
Humor....................0163

Encyclopedia of Jazz.......098

Encyclopedia of Jazz
in the Sixties.............099

Encyclopedia of the
Negro in Africa and
America...................0216

Encyclopedia of the
Negro, Preparatory
Volume with Reference
Lists and Reports.........035

Ethnic Studies in
Higher Education.........0112

Fine Arts and the
Black American...........0102

Government Publications
on the Negro in
America, 1948-1968........055

Graduate and Profes-
sional School
Opportunities for
Minority Students........0117

Graduate Study Oppor-
tunities for Minority
Group Students...........0118

Graduates of Predom-
inantly Negro Colleges:
Class of 1964............0114

Great Documents in
Black American
History...............0134

Guide to Black
Politics '72.........0198

Guide to Documents
in the National
Archives for Negro
Studies...............062

Guide to Films
(16mm) About Negroes..0205

Guide to Negro
Periodical Literature..049

Guide to the Study
of the Negro in
American History......0135

Historical Negro
Biographies............023
(for annotation), 037i

The History of the
Negro in Medicine.....037h

I Too Am America:
Documents from 1619
to the Present.......0141
(for annotation), 037j

In Black and White:
Afro-Americans in
Print.................025

In Freedom's Foot-
steps, From the
African Background
to the Civil War......037a

Index to Periodical
Articles By and About
Negroes...............050

Initial Bibliography
of Immigration and
Race..................0180

International
Library of Negro
Life and History...........037

International
Library of Negro
Life and History:
Yearbook...................038

Introduction to
Black Literature in
America....................037f

Jazz Lexicon..............0100

Joint Center for
Political Studies Guide
to Black Politics '72.....0198

Law, Lawyers, and
Social Change; Cases
and Materials on the
Abolition of Slavery,
Racial Segregation,
and Inequality of Edu-
cational Opportunity......0181

Layman's Guide to Negro
History...................0142

Le Roi Jones (Amiri
Baraka) Bibliography......0154

Le Roi Jones (Imamu
Amiri Baraka): A Check-
list of Works By and
About Him.................0148

Living Black American
Authors: A Biographical
Directory.................0217

Memorable Negroes in
Cleveland's Past..........018

Microcard Collection
of Anti-Slavery Propa-
ganda in the Oberlin
College Library..........0186

Minorities in the
Armed Forces; A
Selected Occasionally
Annotated Bibliography.0193

Minority Groups and
Housing; A Biblio-
graphy, 1950-1970......0191

Minority Groups and
Housing; A Selected
Bibliography, 1950-67..0200

Multimedia Materials
for Afro-American
Studies................0120

Music and the Black
American...............0102

National Black
Business Directory
1971...................0107

National Minority
Business Directory,
1972...................0108

National Profile of
Black Youth: The
Class of 1971..........0124

Negro; A List of
Significant Books.......068

Negro; A Selected
List for School
Libraries of Books......079

Negro Almanac (1st.
ed.)...................042

Negro Almanac (2nd.
ed.)...................043

Negro Americans in
the Civil War.........037b

Negro and Puerto
Rican in American
History...............0137

Negro and the
Establishment:
Law, Politics and
the Courts................0194

Negro Catholic Writers,
1900-1943, a Bio-
bibliography..............0161

Negro Handbook
(1942-49)..................039

Negro Handbook (1966)......034

Negro Heritage............021

Negro History, 1553-
1903; An Exhibition
of Books, Prints, and
Manuscripts........011 & 0140

Negro in America: A
Bibliography (1st. ed.)....063

Negro in America: A
Bibliography (2nd. ed.)....064

Negro in American
Drama....................0103

Negro in American
Literature and a
Bibliography of
Literature By and
About Negro Americans.....0147

Negro in Business--
1936; A Bibliography......0110

Negro in Contemporary
American Literature; An
Outline for Individual
and Group Study..........0152

Negro in Music and Art....037d

Negro in Print............069

Negro in Schoolroom
Literature................0121

Negro in the United
States: A Biblio-
graphy.................058

Negro in the United
States: A Research
Guide..................084

Negro in the United
States: A Selected
Bibliography...........073

Negro Newspapers and
Periodicals in the
United States,
1935-1940..............0174

Negro Newspapers on
Microfilm; A Selected
List...................0173

Negro Novel in America.0146

Negro Population,
1790-1915..............0209

Negro Women Bachelors:
A Comparative Explora-
tion of the Experiences
and Expectations of
College Graduates......0115

Negro Year Book, An
Annual Encyclopedia
of the Negro...........040

Negroes and Mexican
Americans in South and
East Los Angeles;
Changes Between 1960
and 1965...............0192

Negroes in Science:
Natural Science
Doctorates, 1876-1969..0119

Negroes in the United
States; A Bibliography
of Materials for
Schools................080

Negroes in the United
States, 1920-1932........0210

New Jersey and the
Negro; A Bibliography,
1715-1966..................070

News Sheet of the
Charles F. Heartman
Collection.................06

No Crystal Stair; A
Bibliography of Black
Literature.................072

North American Negro
Poets, A Bibliographical
Checklist of Their
Writings, 1760-1944.......0159

100 Amazing Facts About
the Negro.................045

Philadelphia Colored
Directory.................046

Politics of Black
America: An Annotated
Bibliography.............0202

Professional Guide to
the Afro-American in
Print....................077

Psychology of the
Black American...........0207

Quest for Equality:
From Civil War to
Civil Rights.............037c

Race and Region, A
Descriptive Bibliography..0183

Race Relations; A
Selected List of
Readings.................0184

Race Restrictive
Covenants; A Selected
List of References.......0178

Research Reports
(National Scholarship
Service for Negro
Students)..............0124

Segregation and
Desegregation, A
Digest of Recent
Research...............0208

Select Bibliography
of the Negro American...056

Select List of
References on the
Negro Question.........082

Selected Bibliography
for Inter-Racial
Understanding.........0177

Selected Bibliography
on the Negro (3rd. ed.).065

Selected Bibliography
on the Negro (4th. ed.).066

Selected List of
Periodicals Relating
to Negroes............0176

Selected List of
References Relating
to the Elementary,
Secondary, and Higher
Education of Negroes,
1949 to June, 1955.....0127

Selected List of
References Relating
to the Negro Teacher,
1949 to June, 1955.....0128

Selective List of
Government Publica-
tions About the
American Negro
(1969 ed.)............075

Selective List of
Government Publica-
tions About the
American Negro (1970 ed.)..076

Slice of Black
Americana: A Regional
Survey of History, a
Chronology of Publica-
tions from 1746 to 1940...0162

Sociology of the
American Negro...........0206

Source Materials on the
Urban Negro in the
United States: 1910-
1937.....................067

Southampton Slave
Revolt of 1831, a
Compilation of Source
Material.................0188

Southern Black: Slave
and Free; A Biblio-
graphy of Anti- and Pro-
Slavery Books and
Pamphlets................0187

State Universities
and Black Americans:
An Inquiry Into
Desegregation and
Equity for Negroes in
100 Public Universities...0113

Statistical Summary,
State by State, of
School Segregation-
Desegregation............0126

Subject Index to
Literature on Negro
Art......................048

Third Ear: A Black
Glossary.................0203

Up From Within: Today's
New Black Leaders.........020

Voice of Black
America; Major
Speeches in the
United States,
1797-1971..............0136

Who's Who in
Colored America........028

Who's Who in the
American Negro Press...0170

Who's Who of Jazz.......097

Working Bibliography
on the Negro in the
United States..........074

World's Great Men
of Color...............024

Young Negro Talent;
Survey of the
Experiences and
Expectations of
Negro Americans
Who Graduated from
College in 1961........0116

SUBJECT INDEX

Actors.................037e

African
  Literature-
    Bibliography...077, 0155
  Periodicals-
    Directories.........010
  Religion-
    Bibliography.......0211

Africans
  Biographical
    sketches............024

Area Studies
  Bibliography..........061

Art
  Bibliography........0102
  Encyclopedias.......037d

Artists
  Biography-
    Bibliography........0102
  Directories.........0102

Athletes
  Bibliography........0104
  Biography-
    Bibliography........0104

Athletics
  Encyclopedias........037g

Audio-Visual Aids
  Bibliography........057,
    081, 0120, 0138, 0139

Authors
  Bibliography..............09
  Biographical
    sketches....023, 0145, 0217
  Biography-
    Bibliography.....0147, 0165
  Historical time
    line charts............022

Awards....................033

Baraka, Imamu, Amiri
  Bibliography......0148, 0154
  Book Reviews-
    Bibliography.....0148, 0154

Biographical Sketches......08,
  016, 020, 021, 022, 023, 024,
  027, 028, 037, 041, 042, 044,
  097

Biography
  Bibliography............010,
    012, 017, 025

Black Muslims
  Bibliography.......087, 0194

Black Panthers
  Moving Pictures-
    Bibliography..........0205

Black Studies
  Audio-visual Aids-
    Bibliography..........0120
  Bibliography......0120, 0129
  Centers & Programs-
    Directories.......060, 0112
  Course Manuals.........0125

Blues Singers
  Biographical
    sketches...............098

Book Reviews
  Indexes...............047

Booksellers and
Bookselling
  Directories..........0167

Brazilian Literature
  Bibliography..........09

Broadsides
  Bibliography....015, 0159

Brown vs. Board of
Education of
Topeka............093, 0181

Business Enterprises
  Directories....0107, 0108

Caribbean Literature
  Bibliography.........0155

Chicago-Black Americans
  Almanacs..............<u>044</u>
  Biographical
    sketches............044
  Education-
    Bibliography.......0129

Children's Literature
  Bibliography....<u>051</u>, 0121

Civil Rights
  Act of 1957...........093
  Acts of 1960 &
    1964............093, 094
  Associations,
    Institutions, etc. .016,
    033, 042, 089, 0109,0143
  Chronology.......089, 094
  Clippings, Court
    Briefs, Letters,
    etc.-Bibliography....090
  Documents........<u>093</u>, 094
  Education............091
  Leaders-Biographical
    sketches............089
  Moving Pictures-
    Bibliography.......0205
  U.S. Supreme Court
    Decisions...........091

Clergy
  Biographical
    sketches..........<u>029</u>, <u>030</u>
  Geographic Index........<u>030</u>

Cleveland-Black Americans
  Biographical
    sketches............018

College Graduates
  Statistics.............<u>0114</u>,
    <u>0115</u>, <u>0116</u>, <u>0119</u>

Comparative Studies
  Blacks & Whites........<u>0201</u>

Composers
  Bibliography...........09

Courts
  Bibliography.........0194

Cuban Literature
  Bibliography...........09

Cullen, Countee P.
  Bio-Bibliography.......<u>0158</u>
  Book Reviews-
    Bibliography.........0158

Culture
  Bibliography.........<u>01</u>, <u>06</u>

Dancing..................037e

Democratic National
Convention, 1972.........0198

Desegregation in
Education................<u>0113</u>
  Research..............<u>0208</u>
  Statistics........0113, 0126

Dialect
  Bibliography.........0183

Diplomats
  Biographical
    sketches............023

Discrimination
   Bibliography....092, <u>0178</u>
   Education-
      Statistics..........0126
   Employment-
      Bibliography........0106
   Housing-
      Bibliography..0191, 0200
   Moving Pictures......0205

Dissertations,
Academic
Bibliography.......<u>085</u>, <u>086</u>

Documents...<u>093</u>, <u>0134</u>, <u>0141</u>
   Civil Rights....<u>093</u>, <u>094</u>

Douglass, Frederick
   Bibliography..........<u>07</u>

Drama
   Bibliography...<u>0101</u>, <u>0103</u>
   Encyclopedias.......<u>037e</u>

Du Bois, W.E.B.
   Bibliography...0149, <u>0214</u>

Dunbar, Paul
   Lawrence.............0156

Economic Conditions
   Bibliography........<u>0106</u>
   Statistics...........<u>032</u>

Entertainers
   Bibliography........0104
   Biography-
      Bibliography.......0104

Ethnic Studies
   Bibliography....<u>060</u>, <u>0112</u>
   Centers-
      Directories..........060

Family
   Bibliography........0190

Fiction
   Bibliography...0149, 0166

Folk-lore
   African-Bibliography......04
   Bibliography......<u>0153</u>, 0164
   Encyclopedias...........0163

Folk Music
   Bibliography............0153
   Encyclopedias...........0163
   West Indian-
      Discography.............013

Freedom Rides
   Bibliography............087

Garvey, Marcus
   Bibliography............087

Government Publications
   Bibliography............<u>055</u>,
   <u>075</u>, <u>076</u>

Great Britain
   Immigration-
      Bibliography..........0180
   Race Relations-
      Bibliography..........0180

High School Graduates
   Statistics..............<u>0124</u>

History
   Audio-visual Aids-
      Bibliography.....0138, 0139
   Chronology..<u>0130</u>, <u>0133</u>, 0143
   Encyclopedias.....037a, b, c
   Guides to Research0131, <u>0135</u>
   Time Line Charts........<u>022</u>

Housing
   Bibliography......<u>0191</u>, <u>0200</u>

Hughes, Langston
   Bio-Bibliography........<u>0151</u>

Immigration
   Bibliography............<u>0180</u>

Inequality
   Education..............0181
   Statistics..............<u>0179</u>

Intelligence
  Bibliography.........0207
  Comparative
    studies............0201

Jazz Music
  Bibliography...0102, 0105
  Dictionaries........0100
  Discography..........013
  Encyclopedias....098, 099

Jazz Musicians
  Biographical
    sketches...097, 098, 099
  History and
    Criticism-
    Bibliography........0105

Johnson, James
  Weldon..............0156

Jones, Le Roi
  Bibliography...0148, 0154

Journalists
  Biographical
    sketches...........0170

King, Martin Luther, Jr.
  Bibliography.........087
  Speech
    (I have a dream).....093

Landmarks..............042

Language
  Bibliography........0183
  Comparative studies..0201

Law
  Bibliography........0194

Literature
  Bibliography.........09,
    012, 013, 0155, 0160, 0166
  Chronology.........0166
  Encyclopedias.........037f
  Historical Time Line
    Charts................022
  History and Criticism-
    Bibliography....0147, 0165
  Periodicals-
    Directories.....0157, 0172

Los Angeles-
Black Americans
  Statistics............0192

Lynching
  Bibliography...........087
  Statistics.............087

McKay, Claude...........0156

Manuscripts
  Bibliography.....06, 08, 012

Medical Care.............037h

Meredith, James
  Bibliography............087

Migration-Internal
  Bibliography............078

Minnesota-Black Americans
  History-
    Bibliography..........0144

Minstrels
  Bibliography...........0102

Monuments................042

Moving Pictures..........037e
  Bibliography..057, 060, 0205

Music
    African-Discography...013
    Bibliography...0102, 0153
    09
    Encyclopedias........037d
    Historical Time Line
    Charts..............022

Musical Reviews,
Comedies, etc.
    Bibliography........0101

Musicians
    Bibliography........0102
    Biographical
    sketches...097, 098, 099

Nationalism
    Bibliography........0194

New Jersey-
Black Americans
    Bibliography.........070

Newspapers............0175
    Directories..........036,
    0167, 0168, 0171, 0173,
    0174
    Minnesota-
    Directories........0144

New York African
Free School............022

New York City-
Black Americans
    Education-
    Bibliography........0129

Parks, Gordon
    Bibliography........0149

Periodical Articles
    Analytics.........02, 09

Periodicals...........0175
    Directories.........010,
    016, 0143, 0160, 0169,
    0174, 0176

Philadelphia-
Black Americans...........046
    Churches................046
    Literature..............046
    Population (1907).......046

Philosophers
    Biographical
    sketches..............0197

Philosophy
    Bibliography...........0197

Poetry..............036, 0156
    Bibliography......0150, 0159

Police
    Bibliography...........0194

Political Conventions
    Delegates..............0198

Politics..................0198
    Bibliography..04, 0194, 0202

Population
    Congressional
    Districts-
    Statistics.............0198
    Statistics.............032,
    034, 036, 0198, 0209, 0210

Portraits................018,
    024, 028, 035, 036, 037,
    041, 042, 043, 044, 045,
    052, 097, 098, 099, 0107,
    0108, 0134, 0151, 0175, 0212

Prejudice
    Bibliography............092

Press Services
    Directories............0174

Primary Sources
    Bibliography............014

Professional Education
    Directories............0117

Public Officials
  Bibliography.........026
  Biographical
    sketches............019
  Southern States......0204

Publishers and Publishing
  Directories.........0167

Psychology
  Bibliography........0207

Race-Biological Aspects
  Bibliography........0207

Race Relations
  Bibliography....060, 0180

Radio.................0175

Radio Stations
  Directories.........0167

Religion...............036
  Bibliography...0182, 0211
  Racism..............0139

Research Guides.......063,
    064, 084
  History........0131, 0135

Scholarships............033

Scientists
  Biography-
    Bibliography........026
  Directories..........026

Segregation
  Bibliography........0206
  Court Cases.........0181
  Education-
    Statistics.........0126
  Research.............0208

Sit-ins
  Bibliography.........087

Slang
  Dictionaries...........0100,
    0199, 0203

Slavery
  Autobiographies-
    Bibliography............09
  Narratives-
    Bibliography.......09, 0186
  Revolts.................0188

Social Conditions
  Bibliography............063

Sociology
  Bibliography...........0206

South American Blacks
  Biographical
    sketches..............024

Southampton Slave Revolt..0188

Southern Students
Protest Movement
  Bibliography............087

Speeches, Addresses, etc..0136

Spirituals
  Bibliography......0102, 0153

Statistics.................032,
    039, 040, 042, 043, 0143

Teachers
  Bibliography...........0128

Television................037e

United Nations-Embassies
  African.................0167
  Caribbean...............0167

United States Congress
  Black Membership........0198
  Civil Rights............089

Universities and Colleges
  Directories....0123, 0167
  Graduate Study-
  Directories...0117, 0118

Urban Life
  Bibliography.........067
  Moving Pictures-
  Bibliography........0205

Voting
  Bibliography..........04
  Voting Rights
  Act of 1965.........094

Washington, Booker T.
  Bibliography.........087

West Indian Literature
  Bibliography.....09, 0155

West Indian Poetry
  Bibliography........0159

West Indians
  Biographical
  sketches............024
  Migration-
  Bibliography........0180

Wit and Humor
  Encyclopedias........0163

Women
  Authors-
  Bibliography........0190
  Bibliography...0190, 0212
  Biography-
  Bibliography..0190, 0212
  College Graduates-
  Statistics.........0114,
  0115, 0119
  Fine Arts
  Bibliography.......0212
  Social Sciences
  Bibliography........0212

Women's Liberation
  Bibliography........0190

Wright, Richard
  Bibliography...........0149

91803